Rae Ea

YOUR BRAIN NEEDS

a hug

Life, Love, Mental Health,
and Sandwiches

[Imprint]
MAKE YOUR MARK

New York

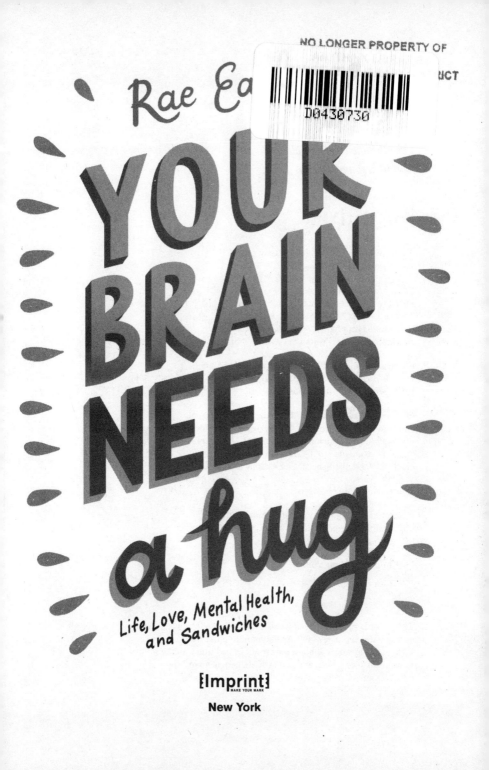

For all those lovely people who
help to keep me healthy.

[Imprint]
MAKE YOUR MARK

A part of Macmillan Publishing Group, LLC
120 Broadway, New York, NY 10271

YOUR BRAIN NEEDS A HUG
LIFE, LOVE, MENTAL HEALTH, AND SANDWICHES
Text copyright © 2019 by Rae Earl
Illustrations copyright © 2018 by Jo Harrison
All rights reserved. Printed in the United States of America.

Library of Congress Control Number: 2018955995
ISBN 978-1-250-30785-9 (paperback)
ISBN 978-1-250-30786-6 (ebook)

Our books may be purchased in bulk for promotional,
educational, or business use. Please contact your local
bookseller or the Macmillan Corporate and Premium
Sales Department at (800) 221-7945 ext. 5442 or by
email at MacmillanSpecialMarkets@macmillan.com.

Illustrations by Jo Harrison

Imprint logo designed by Amanda Spielman
Originally published in the United Kingdom
by Wren and Rook in 2017

First Imprint edition, 2019
10 9 8 7 6 5 4 3 2 1

fiercereads.com

This guide is protected by universal warm vibes of brain calmness
and occasional bursts of joy. Any attempt to upset this book by
saying unkind words about it may result in bad tunes on the radio,
showers on your picnic, and, worst of all, people giving you
melon as an appetizer.

THIS IS A BOOK ABOUT MY BRAIN, YOUR BRAIN, AND HOW TO LOOK AFTER IT.

Plus random pieces of possibly useful advice about life, love, cats, and sandwich toppings.

CONTENTS

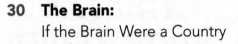

WHAT THIS BOOK IS ABOUT . . .

This is a book about brains. First, it's about my brain and how I have managed to train it like a magnificent puppy who occasionally rips up the sofa but mainly does as it's told. It's also about the specific things that can go wrong with all of our heads and how I think you can best handle them.

Everything in this book is based on my experiences. Sometimes good friends and family have let me tell their stories too, but mainly it's about my head. All the things I've learned have kind of been learned the hard way. That's fine, though—I think my experiences might help you or just make you feel a little bit more comfortable in your own head.

There's a lot of content in this book that for many people is going to be confronting and triggering. You'll probably know what kind of subjects may be very sensitive to you. Can I suggest just taking it really slowly and, if anything alarms you or upsets you, talk to someone you trust? If it feels like it's getting to be too much, just stop reading and come back to the book when you feel stronger. I'm not going anywhere and I can wait. Good advice usually makes the best impact at a good time.

Anyway . . .

I thought I'd start with something that happened last week. It's reminded me of one very important thing . . .

Looking After Your Head Is a Lifelong Thing. And That's FINE.

I cried about this book when I went to the doctor. She's lovely. I said, "I'm writing a book trying to help people manage their brains when I can't even manage mine properly. I woke up this morning with my heart trying to rip itself away from my rib cage in panic. I'm a mess. Everyone thinks I'm coping with this. Except certain members of my family. I've told them because they guessed. They know me. But I'm a mess. A MESS. What if I tell people the wrong thing and, oh—I'm sorry. I've just broken your desk calendar fiddling with it. Sorry. SORRY."

My doctor *(four kids, really funny, tremendous boots-tights combo every time I see her)* said, "It's strange, isn't it? We don't do anything much for our brains. We spend hours in a gym trying to get really good thighs, yet we don't pay much attention to our brains. What are we doing to help the thing that's in charge of everything?"

(I'm sniffing and nodding through all of this. I can't see the tissues.) "Sometimes," she continued, "people come in here and they are really struggling. And I want to make them better, but I can't always do that. All we can do is our best. We make mistakes. We are human."

(Massive nose blow from me. I've located the tissues.)

I then asked my doctor if I could steal this, because it's actually a brilliant place to start the book. She said yes and didn't ask for any payment, so here we are.

She's right. Most of us don't look after our head until something goes wrong. Yet taking care of our brain is the single most important thing we can do for our entire existence on this earth, and on other planets. (I'm hoping this book will be in print for a while.)

Science and medicine move on, but some things are timeless. Before we start properly, I want to remind you of one REALLY. VITAL. THING.

YOU ARE HUMAN.

YOU are descended from apes.

YOU are part of a race that we still don't fully understand. We understand polar bears better than we understand ourselves. That's how weird we are.

YOU are not perfect. Sloths and anteaters are perfect.

You will NEVER be as perfect as them because you are HUMAN.

You're human. It might seem like an obvious thing to say, but it's worth saying again. Not so long ago in the history of this universe, your ancestors were apes in trees. Yet right now a great deal is probably being asked of you that was never asked of them. There is no fossilized evidence to suggest that gorillas took exams or had to negotiate social media. There is pressure on you—at home, in education, at work, in relationships—EVERYWHERE. You HAVE to remember you are human—magnificent but flawed. Your life, like all human lives, will be marked by your strength and your frailty, by your good times and your bad times. If sometimes you find it hard to cope, that's normal.

Give yourself a break. Really.

There are very few mistakes that are so dreadful we can't recover from them. Bad times really do pass, and you can survive a great deal even if you are a quivering jelly wreck while doing so.

But PLEASE be kind to yourself. I will keep repeating this.

GIVE YOURSELF A BREAK.

In fact, my magnificent illustrator, Jo, can you make that phrase into a glorious coat of arms, please, that can be returned to at any point? Particularly at moments of immense personal hell, anxiety, and strain? I need it, for a start.

Thank you, Jo. You're clever.

I'm going to do "good," "bad," and "ugly" emotions in this book. It's important we are honest. I'm giving myself a massive break and assuming at least ONE person reading this might know exactly where I am coming from. I hope it's you, and you get something from it. I hope it's something that helps the part of life you're currently traveling through feel a little easier. I've broken the book down into different chapters so, like a private beach in Malibu that only YOU are allowed to go on, you can dip in and out at your leisure.

HOW THE HELL ARE YOU? NO. WHO THE HELL AM I?

How are you?

I don't mean in the "Yes! I'm fine, I've got a brilliant weekend coming up if I can just get everything done and isn't this rain awful? I blame global warming" kind of way.

I mean how are YOU really? What's going on inside?

As you can see from my doctor's visit, I've got quite a lot going on at the moment, and you may well be thinking, how can THAT help ME? Good question.

This is my introduction as to why I think I might be

qualified to help anyone, and it isn't because I think I've got ALL the answers. I haven't.

I haven't got a psychology degree either. My experience with the psychiatric profession has been solely as a patient. Not always a good patient either. I once tried to throw a typewriter at a child psychiatrist. I haven't always wanted help, even though I needed it. If I'm being honest, my life has been full of some quite spectacular failures and some truly epic errors of judgment. I've made an utter DICK of myself frankly. And my head. Oh, this head. It's been a mess. Some days (see doctor incident) it still wants to be, BUT . . .

It's because of ALL this I might be able to help.

I'm writing this in a shed 10,500 miles from the house I used to HAVE to stay in. The house I was trapped in by anxiety, crippling OCD, jibes about my weight, my own sabotaging thoughts, and a head and body that REALLY seemed to HATE me. For years and years, my emotions were on a constant "self-destruct" setting.

At sixteen years old, I was in a psychiatric ward after a complete nervous breakdown. I should have been doing what I perceived to be "normal" stuff—like going to parties and doing hot stuff with hot guys. Instead I was doing exercises with mini beanbags and group therapy sessions with people twenty years older than me.

Luckily, therapy has evolved a lot since the mini beanbags, and the counseling I've had as an adult hasn't involved anything cushion-related at all. Unless I'm holding one to my tummy for comfort . . .

(I do this ALL the time. Apparently, this is because when we were apes the stomach was the most exposed part of the body. If you do that too, you are not being weird. You are just protecting yourself should you end up in the rain forest again. See? Our brains are a completely baffling milkshake of evolution, experience, and other stuff that we can't really explain.)

When I was younger, I was REALLY ill. I didn't know my conditions had a name then. I just thought I was EVIL and I was being punished. I thought I was the Messiah, or the devil, or at least someone who had complete control of world events and the careers of musicians. My brain screamed awful thoughts at me. I'd see someone I loved and my brain would flash an image of them dying horribly or having really nasty sex. I'd punish these thoughts by self-harming. I thought I could prevent wars by checking the front door thirty-six times. I was medically obese because I self-medicated with things that became issues in themselves. Like a crap sponge cake, I added layer upon layer of problems. I soothed my crushing anxiety with chocolate bars and intravenous toast with half a tub of cheese spread per slice. All this was going on while I was trying to finish school essays AND while the "child" psychiatrist was encouraging me to draw my life "as a garden with an unsupportive trellis." I think that's when I tried to throw the typewriter. It was too heavy, though—this was before lightweight MacBook Pros, which are a lot easier to use in anger.

To the outside, however, I was a big grin. A sack of silly. This was partly the real me and partly a way to mask the fact I felt dreadful. Unhinged most of the time. I was MUCH worse than I was telling ANYONE—including the medical staff. I didn't really come clean about how I felt or what I thought for YEARS. I was too scared to. Scared they'd lock me up forever or put me in prison or take me to be part of a secret government scheme to test drugs on. You can tell already that I was REALLY into catastrophizing.

Catastrophizing is a terrible thing. It's what psychologists call "thinking traps." There's a few of these. The mind can get stuck into ways of thinking very quickly. For example "all or nothing" thinking, where everything in the world appears completely black or white, or "confirmation bias," where we find evidence to support our beliefs and ignore any facts that may contradict them. (This is what my mom does with her theory on ghosts!)

These traps can snare your head. Catastrophizing is a nasty one. It turns a small issue into something HUGE and makes situations seem completely unfixable. It's a broken express escalator of bad thoughts that takes you from the top floor and plummets you to the very bottom. The worst scenario is ALWAYS the one that you are convinced is going to happen.

For example:

8TH FLOOR   I've got my English exam on Monday.

7TH FLOOR   I am going to get into the exam room and know nothing.

6TH FLOOR   I am going to sit there for hours and have to fiddle with my pen and know nothing.

5TH FLOOR   People will stare at me as I fail.

4TH FLOOR   I am going to fail and I won't be able to get into college.

3RD FLOOR   I am going to fail and I won't be able to get a job.

2RD FLOOR   I will probably end up having to do something really dangerous for a living just to pay the rent.

1ST FLOOR   Something so dangerous I will be horribly injured.

GROUND   Or die.

BASEMENT   I'm going to fail my English exam and I'm going to die. Everything is a mess.

My life was full of that type of thinking. I felt like I was ALWAYS falling and failing.

The reason I've told you all this is that I want to tell you one very important thing.

It's ended up OK. I'm OK.

I had to find ways to cope and ways to get better. The truth is, I still have to use those methods sometimes. It's not unusual. Everyone has mental struggles they have to learn to deal with. I did and I do. I want to share my brain with you. Not because I think I have the magic wand of IN-STANT MIND RELIEF. I'm not a miracle worker. I just think I "get" some head stuff and what I've learned along the way might help you to enjoy YOUR life a bit more. I think I might be able to suggest some ways to make YOUR life a bit better. And YOU matter. You matter to your friends, to your family, and to us all. You probably have no idea what you are capable of.

BUT I'm not a doctor, and doctors, counselors, psychologists, and psychiatrists are by and large lovely people who don't deserve to have any writing implement of any description thrown at them. That's why, if you're feeling ill, or if you are slightly suspicious that your brain isn't working as well as it should be, OR you are just curious about how to keep your brain healthy, I want you to go and see your doctor. I STILL DO when I feel bad, as I have proved! There's ZERO shame in it. I PROMISE they've heard it all before and much, MUCH worse. And if you don't like the first doctor you see, ask to see another. Just please go. Don't waste years like I did, and then see something on *The Oprah Winfrey Show* and realize you're not Satan but actually someone suffering from a mental health problem. What a waste. Learn from my mess. Go and see a professional. We've got one here in this book actually—Dr. Radha (aka Dr. R.). She will be sharing her years of experience and her amazing skills in this book too. She's the sort of doctor I wish my teenage brain had had access to. She's kind, she's clever, and she GETS it.

For my part, let me spill my guts and fill in what some people call the "treatment gap" a bit. That's the space between you feeling bad and you seeing a doctor.

All this is just how I see it and how I've experienced it, so please cut me some slack. I don't always come across that well. I'm fine with that. For me it's another way to make sense of what I've experienced and to give my past mental health problems a bit of a silver lining. Mainly I'm doing it because I hate the thought of another Rae/Ray stuck in a dreadful head place that they can't get out of. That's how I felt, but there *was* a way out. I just needed help to find it.

Not everything here may be relevant to you, but spread it around if it's not. If it doesn't affect you, I can almost guarantee it affects someone you know. Mental health problems are not rare, and they don't discriminate. Mental well-being and keeping our brains healthy, resilient, and in a good place is relevant to us ALL. You will help everyone if you spread this message on.

Now, I want to start with two universal things that I think everyone should know.

Aircraft Emergencies and the Best Piece of Advice You'll Ever Get

I'm a geek. I was a geek before it was trendy to be one, and I had to practice in secret. Apparently I'm on some sort of spectrum (I reject this—see "How to Wear Your Diagnosis" later).

The truth is, I'm a plane spotter.

When mentally well enough, I used to scrape myself up to the viewing platforms at Heathrow. Then I'd have a day of Kit Kats and nonstop aviation action. I still go to the end of the runway at Hobart airport some Sunday afternoons and sit under the flight path. I have an app where I can see all the world's air traffic at once. I LOVE planes. LOVE them. I can recognize most of the world's airlines from their tail fins and most plane types from JUST THEIR WINGS. No.

Don't close this book.

Don't leave.

Don't go. PLEASE. This isn't about what you think it is and we all have secret pleasures. (They aren't guilty by the way, unless they are damaging you or someone else. Guilty pleasures are NONSENSE. They are just PLEASURES.)

I promise I won't discuss my favorite uniform of all time (although it's obviously Japan Airlines' classic crane—all the retro chic), and I'll try not to bore you. I just want to give you the greatest piece of advice about life you will EVER get, which comes from flying.

And that is . . .

Put your own oxygen mask on before helping others

Assuming you're not reading this at 36,000 feet in the middle of a midair emergency, you might be wondering what I'm talking about.

It struck me about sixteen years ago. I was on a plane to Dubai, and they kept showing a safety video featuring this woman putting on her own oxygen mask before helping her sweet, angelic-looking kid. I was outraged. I said to my husband, "WHAT SORT OF MOTHER THINKS ABOUT HER OWN OXYGEN SUPPLY BEFORE THINKING ABOUT HER CUTE, TEDDY-BEAR-HOLDING DAUGHTER?!" The tiny child was probably gasping for air, like a goldfish whipped out of a garden pond by a cat, and the mother LOOKED AFTER HERSELF FIRST.

And he pointed out that that was right.

Totally right.

Because unless she made sure she was OK first, she wouldn't be able to help anyone else. Including the people she loved the most. I was a newlywed at this point and concerned I'd married a sociopath. But I hadn't. I'd married someone with immense emotional common sense who was inadvertently a bit bloody Zen magnificent.

I am not naturally Zen. In fact, I have created the opposite to Zen. It is Nez. I am Nez. However I have learned some of the ways of the naturally calm, and so can you.

Put your own oxygen mask on before helping others

This is exactly the same for you in your life.

You cannot help anyone if you don't help yourself. You deserve to feel good. You need to get your brain in the best state possible FOR YOU. It's not for your friends, your parents, your exam results, your partner, your future career as president of the USA . . .

Work out your motivation for wanting to be better. It could be lots of reasons, but bring it back to YOU. You're doing this for YOU. So you can enjoy life in the best way possible and survive the bad times. This is your responsibility and, the great news is, by doing it you also help the people around you. Looking after your head is not a selfish act. It's an act of someone who wants to survive and contribute to the world they live in.

Dr. R. says: *In actual fact, a lot of the time, once you start practicing self-care and love, you will often find people around you may also start looking after themselves. Actions really do speak louder than words, and often the most powerful thing we can do for other people is to practice what we are preaching. Habits are contagious, and it is surprising what happens to the people around you when you start. Try it out and see!*

Put yourself first. YOU deserve it.

Oh, and if you are involved in a real-life aircraft emergency, count the seats to the nearest exit, listen to the crew announcements, and:

Put your own oxygen mask on before helping others

Tiny anxiety management tip—a little preparation and information soothes paranoia. Too much can stoke it. A small amount is generally all you need.

Listen to the recording (it's on YouTube) of the air traffic controller at Heathrow handling the crash of British Airways Flight 38 in 2008. If you want to hear how fantastic brains can be under pressure, that's the bit of audio you need. Every person involved makes their mind work magnificently. All the air traffic controllers. The pilot of the crashed plane. The flight crew. The fire engine crew. The guy flying the Qatar Airways flight who was just about to land, had to abort, and "go around." EVERYONE in that situation was human and brilliant. There is no reason that your mind can't be trained, tamed, and exercised to work as well as theirs. Don't be told you are limited by your brain. I was told that by a few people. It's proved to be totally false. No one has a crystal ball about your future. Where you are now is NOT a life sentence. As previously discussed, I am naturally Nez, but I have learned the ways of Zen-ish.

Pssst! The Biggest Secret You'll Never Get Told

Second big thing.

It can be incredibly lonely being you. You look around and everyone else seems to have it sorted out. People are being hilarious on Twitter and you're not. There are sharp cheekbones and incredible eye makeup all over Instagram. Everyone is having a brilliant time and you're in your bedroom watching *Cruel Intentions* on Netflix AGAIN.

(This is all my experience, by the way.)

It's all nonsense, of course, because the biggest secret you'll never get told is that 99 percent of us think we're dicks, and everyone is struggling. Fear of missing out is not a new thing. There are probably ancient cave paintings of a Stone Age man sitting at home looking sad in front of his campfire while the rest of his friends are out clobbering mammoths.

The reason I know this for definite is that when *My Mad Fat Diary* was published, lots of my old classmates got in touch with me. Including a woman I knew as "the Swan." She was BEAUTIFUL. Blond. Skinny even though I saw her demolish a ton of fries on a daily basis. She smelled like the Clarins counter at Christmas and looked like MAC had gotten to her as soon as she got out of bed. She didn't walk. She drifted by like she was on wheels. And no—you don't get a storybook villainess, because she was smart and funny too. I loved her and I hated her because the jealous part of me made me horrible. "If only I could be like her, everything would be fine," I thought.

So *My Mad Fat Diary* came out, and I got a message from her.

She wrote, "I wish I'd known how you felt, because I felt exactly the same way."

You can imagine what my face did. It sort of collapsed. Nah. Really. Come on, Miss Gorgeous. What a load of nonsense. You're just trying to be nice. You were the poster girl for perfect.

I didn't write that, but I thought it. I did feel instantly bad for the bitter brain vomit, but I can tell you that. This isn't a book about fluffy blue-sky-and-rainbow-unicorn thoughts. I have my horrid head moments. We all do. The key thing, though, is that I thought it. I didn't share it.

I actually replied with something like, "Really? I thought you breezed through."

The Swan replied with one of the loveliest things I've ever read.

She said that she wished she'd known I was struggling

because we could have been even closer friends than we were. She'd also experienced those creeping feelings of hating her body and her head. She added detail that made me know it was the truth. She said she'd thought I was super cool and she loved the way I made cocky rugby players feel tiny when they gave me grief. In fact, lots of people thought I'd been a largely splendid teenager.

Perhaps I was, but I didn't see it. All I focused on was the mess. The raging mess and the voices in my head that told me I was nothing. Where did they start? Nowhere I can remember, but they were there, as they are for many of us.

The fact is, we are all just making it up as we go along. Often, we present our lives to others through an Instagram filter, real or imaginary. Mine is naturally "Lark"—it brightens just about everything, but in reality things are duller and often darker. On my Instagram feed the other morning, I posted a picture of a rose with droplets of water on it. (It's still there—have a look if you want to.) The morning looked like a beautiful flower. What the photo didn't show, however, was me shouting at the coffee machine and calling it a "bloody, bloody, BLOODY useless piece of crap" and then putting my trousers on THE WRONG WAY (washing label sticking out, ahoy!) and not noticing till past 10 A.M. I just showed everyone one side of my life. Not all of it.

Everyone is a mess sometimes. Everyone has their moments. The route to every success is paved with failure—that's nothing to be afraid of. Every life has its share of setbacks and mistakes—that's normal.

They are nothing to be afraid of.

If you're messing up, you are trying and you are living and you are learning. It's something we are ALL going through from day to day. Everyone.

As soon as you acknowledge that you are not alone, and that no one has it sorted out really, the world feels . . . fairer. You feel less like the ugly duckling splashing around at the back of the pond while all the swans drift by. Feeling good is not a race or a competition with the people around us. It's a journey we take, sometimes with the help of others and sometimes disregarding others. It's what being human is about, so:

Put your oxygen mask on before helping others

Give yourself a break. I'm keeping it simple because this brain business is very complicated. We're dealing with a bonkers place to visit. That's why it has so many guidebooks.

IF THE BRAIN WERE A COUNTRY

The Brain

If the brain were a country, it would be the most terrifying, complicated, and exciting place on earth. We know bits about it, but not much because we only really discovered it was there recently. Well, we knew it was there, but we thought other countries like the Lung Republic were more important.

Actually the brain is THE most important country on earth. It bosses everything else. A crisis in the country of Brain, and the rolling news would go crazy, because basically everything else in the body world goes bananas.

We are all explorers of this new territory. You'll constantly be discovering. Your brain is unique and it is beautiful. It may also be a total bastard. It can go from an all-inclusive tropical beach resort with a twenty-four-hour buffet to a bombed-out war zone within a matter of minutes. It's a country that needs constant maintenance and a lot of exploration to understand properly. The GREAT news is, the more you start to explore it, the better you know where everything is and how it all works. It's a constant work in progress, but it gets easier the more you practice.

To illustrate this, I've created, with the help of Jo, a cross section of my brain today:

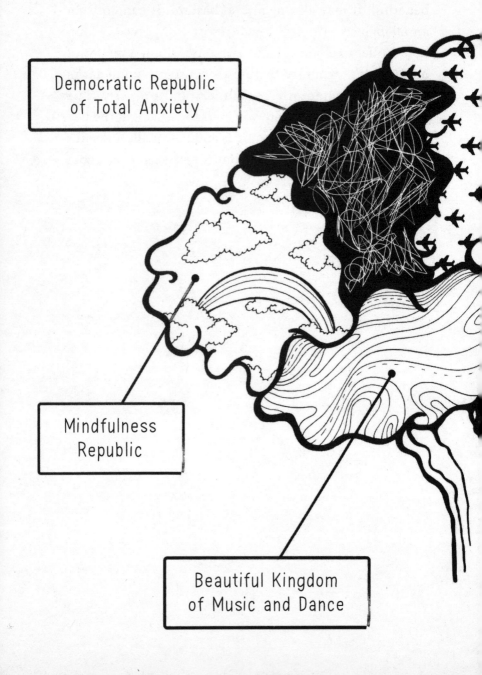

Democratic Republic
of Total Anxiety

Mindfulness
Republic

Beautiful Kingdom
of Music and Dance

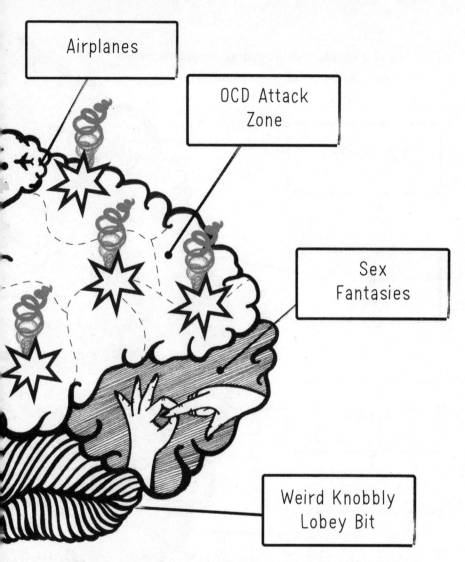

Airplanes

OCD Attack
Zone

Sex
Fantasies

Weird Knobbly
Lobey Bit

You can see by my brain that there are some areas of concern—the OCD Attack Zone and the Democratic Republic of Total Anxiety. But these are kept at bay with my Mindfulness Republic and the Beautiful Kingdom of Music and Dance. This is a trained brain. Primed over years with counseling and hypnotherapy.

Now, this is an illustration of what scientists basically know about your brain. The growing brain:

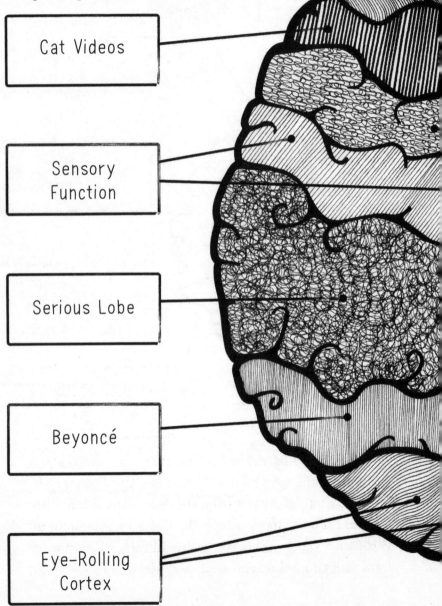

Cat Videos

Sensory Function

Serious Lobe

Beyoncé

Eye-Rolling Cortex

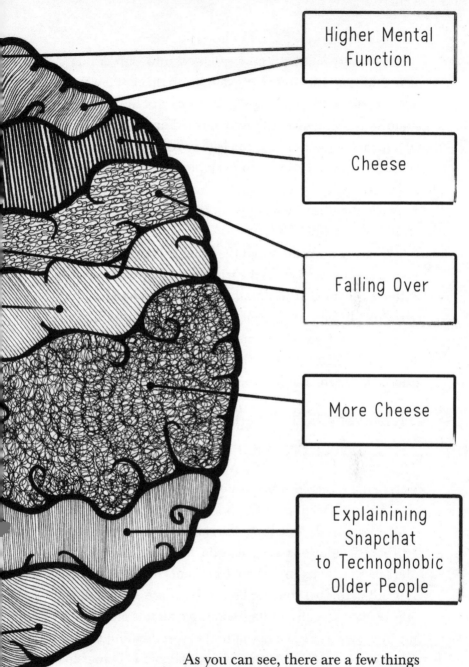

Higher Mental
Function

Cheese

Falling Over

More Cheese

Explainining
Snapchat
to Technophobic
Older People

As you can see, there are a few things
that the medical profession isn't quite sure about.

However, fantastic new research into our minds is being done all the time. For example, in the past few years some research has suggested that the part of the brain that handles consequence isn't fully formed until lots of us are in our early twenties. This can lead to risky and dangerous behavior. I want to write an example here of something I once did involving a freezing-cold golf course in Scotland in November, but I won't just in case someone equally as stupid copies me.

What we do know about the brain between the ages of twelve and twenty is that the wiring can be fundamentally different from that in an adult brain. It's changing and growing all the time. Inevitably this can lead to difficult situations and it's sometimes hard to distinguish between how UTTERLY LOUSY this period can feel for anyone and an acute mental health problem.

Not every bad or negative feeling is a sign your brain is malfunctioning.

It's not. It can just be part of life.

You're allowed to FEEL. Some things cannot be medicated or cured, and they shouldn't be. Some of these "difficult" emotions keep us safe. We need them! They alert us to threats in our environment. If a hungry tiger is heading toward you, anxiety and fear are absolutely the appropriate response! Life isn't always simple and there is no "normal." It's fine and natural to feel dreadful sadness sometimes. That's different from depression. Things like elation, grief, anger, mood swings, and many of the growth patterns and feelings that make adolescence hard are natural. It's your absolute right to experience them. They don't need a label; they are what they are.

You wouldn't be human without them.

The problem is, the world is often at war with this period of growth. I was dismissed as a difficult, hormonal teenager for a LONG time when actually I was very ill. People's attitudes and beliefs can sometimes make it very hard to negotiate this part of your life, and it can also be tricky to work out what sort of care you DO need.

I'm going to go through some things that can go wrong in the brain and what I think makes them feel different from things that are more "standard" parts of everyday life. Please notice I'm doing everything in my power to avoid the word "normal." There is no normal when it comes to brains—different brains at different times just need different degrees of help.

I've experienced some of these things, and I'll talk about how they felt for me and what I did to make them better. (Or, sometimes, what I do NOW to make them better.) I will also be using the experiences of other people who have very kindly said I could write about them. Lots of things can happen to the brain, and lots of people battle with theirs. Whatever odd thing you're thinking, I can almost guarantee someone has thought or is thinking it RIGHT NOW too.

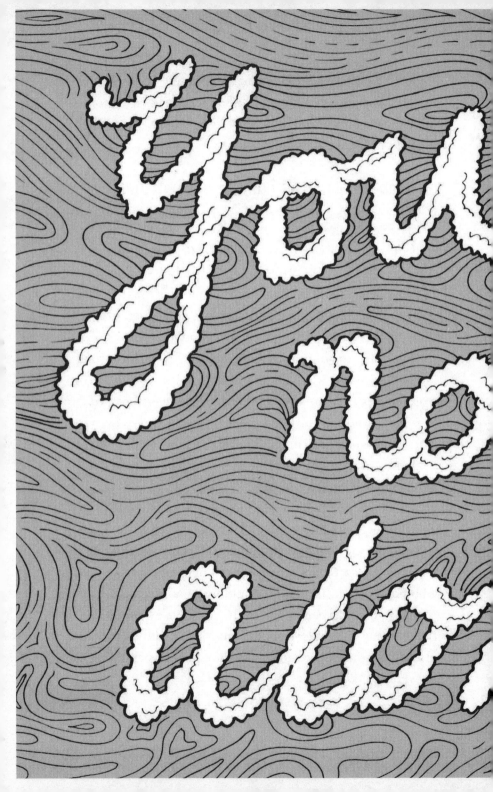

"THERE'S HONESTLY NOTHING WRONG EXCEPT YOU MIGHT DIE"

Anxiety

I try to smile sweetly at people who tell me, "Don't worry," but a terrible part of me wants to pelt them repeatedly in the face with really wet sponges full of cheap shampoo. The sort that renders you temporarily blind when it gets in your eyes.

I know. Nasty. But it's one of those phrases people use to try to make you feel better, and it's useless. We'll cover other pointless but well-meaning phrases later, and I'll probably end up using some—so sorry in advance. It's understandable to get angry and offended by PEOPLE'S TOTAL MISUNDERSTANDING OF EVERYTHING you are going through, but good people say dumb things. You have to give people who are trying to help you a break. And in real life I usually do, but here I can tell you what I really think . . .

Yeah. "Don't worry." ARGH.

How to Handle Your Anxiety

Everyone suffers from anxiety at one time or another. This is because from a very early age we realize that much of the world is beyond our control. I go into how to cope with anxiety later in this chapter, but to begin, I want to talk about anxiety in general.

Some of it appears insane (wars over seemingly nothing, the fact that people are STILL starving, latex leggings, etc.).

We have to find a way to react to it. Anxiety is a natural response to the world.

As I've mentioned above, we can find ourselves in some situations where anxiety can help us. You're probably unlikely to meet a tiger today, but you'll have other worrying situations to deal with. Life can be stressful. It exposes us to new scary situations constantly—exams, relationships, money worries, wars, terrorism, the fact that I've completely forgotten it's my mom's birthday. How on earth could I forget that? She'll wake up tomorrow morning, and there'll be no card or gift and she'll think, NO ONE LOVES ME, and she'll cry.

And OH MY GOD, what if that makes her actually ill? She's had issues with her heart. You hear of these people being hospitalized with actual heartbreak! I can see her now, lying in bed weeping, whispering my name. I'M THE WORST DAUGHTER IN THE WORLD!

There. Right THERE.

Worries. They can spiral into each other. The difference between worry and anxiety is a fundamental one, but it's not always easy to distinguish between the two.

The way I see it, worry has a specific cause. You can look at a worry rationally and you can work out ways to tackle it.

For example:

"I've Forgotten About My Mom's Birthday."

I will message her first thing in the morning and sing "Happy Birthday" to her. She will be thrilled. I will then ask her what she would like for her birthday and arrange it online. I will also give her the greatest gift of all—I will tell her I'm sorry and that I still struggle without her guidance. She will smile broadly from ear to ear and feel loved and needed. Which she is. She will not be hospitalized. I am not in control of her health anyway. She is. She will have an excellent birthday and all will be well.

"I'm the Worst Daughter in the World."

No, I'm not, but I definitely need to invest in a decent calendar or put alerts in my phone.

Worry is legitimate. It happens every so often. Someone you love is ill, you're taking an exam, you have to travel somewhere new and you're unsure. It's a big deal, but when you tackle that worry, the horrible feeling subsides.

You can take a deep breath and deal with the problem, muddle your way through it and cope.

Anxiety is like slowly drowning in your own head. It's beyond worry, and it doesn't stop. Night and day. You tackle one concern, and another one explodes in your brain. You lurch from one disaster to the next. With anxiety, you take a deep breath and there's no air. It's all been ripped away, like a bomb has gone off and taken all the oxygen from the atmosphere. It's impossible to think clearly. You have a very real feeling that things will never be all right again.

Me and Anxiety

But here's the good news. You can get on top of it.

I have been plagued by anxiety for most of my life. It still tries to invade my head and take over. As you know, I nearly gave up this book because I felt like I couldn't write it. Good opportunity here to let the anxious part of my brain take over, so you can see what it whispers to me:

"Publish the book, then! And everyone will say it's crap. Or they will read this bit and think you've put that in there to make sure they say it's not crap. Stop fishing. They'll know. They'll say it's crap anyway because it is.

ANXIETY is like SLOWLY DROWNING in YOUR OWN HEAD

All the reviews. You'll be a laughingstock. You can't help anyone. They know it. They look at you and you KNOW THEY know it. You're flunking this and everyone is going to find out. They'll find out you're a total fraud and that you should be sat back in your bedroom in Stamford doing doodles and listening to Blur. By the way, that pain you have right now? Pancreatic cancer. Definitely. You are—"

WHATEVER, SIR BASTARD OF ANXIETY. WHATEVER. SHUT UP.

So he's still there. Galloping into my head on his mighty steed of terror when I least want him to.

Even writing that made me breathless. But I've developed coping mechanisms to stop him from taking over completely.

First, here are some of the things I did wrong for YEARS (and when I say years, I mean decades):

I didn't tell anyone how I was feeling.

I also fueled and fed my anxiety with information it didn't need.

I poured gasoline on it. I used to research specific horrors to worry about, like nuclear war. I can tell you precisely what happens within a fifteen-mile radius of a one-ton megaton bomb falling. I wasn't in charge of strategic command for the British Army. I didn't need to know. Likewise, I know the precise incubation period of rabies and all the symptoms that come from eating a death cap mushroom.

I used knowledge to fan, rather than allay, my anxiety and when it all got too much (regularly), I would comfort-eat. I self-harmed, because I felt it could pull me out of the panic. (I will talk more about this later.)

I stayed in my bedroom. I could get to school and back, but then I'd disappear upstairs. No socializing. No phone. No contact with anyone, but I was safe. Safe in my bedroom, where nothing bad could happen.

Then, in 1988, a plane exploded over Lockerbie, a little town like mine in Scotland, and I realized you weren't absolutely safe anywhere.

It happened near Christmas. I stayed in bed terrified for a week. My Christmas dinner came up on a tray. I couldn't move. I was trapped in a spiral of doom. I thought a piece of the glass I was drinking from had chipped off and was ripping my insides. I rushed downstairs in a state and started ranting. My poor mom didn't know what to do. She shouted at me, then cried. It's very hard to know how to help someone that ill. I think she made me play a game of Trivial Pursuit and I ate a mince pie, or four.

I was so terrified of both living and dying that my anxiety became a kind of living death. It was an existence, but nothing more than that. I was on something terrible that I couldn't get off. I felt like I was always hurtling toward disaster.

I wasn't, of course. It took some time, but I managed to start living. It was small steps at first, but while writing this, I've just removed a lizard from the shed that I'm writing in. I didn't think I'd be tackling reptiles abroad. Ever. I had trouble getting to the grocery store.

Here are some of the symptoms of anxiety:

Your heart can race and you can have chest pains that shoot into your jaw and arm. This feels like a heart attack, or a really tight, badly fitting bra.

Your entire body can go tingly and numb. I had a doctor visit me in a vacation home in Cornwall once because I was convinced I was having a stroke. I'd read that the nearest hospital was twenty minutes away. I had it in my head that if I got appendicitis it would burst somewhere on the A30 before I got to the hospital. I would die and lots of people in incredible swimwear would have their day at the seaside ruined. I could see them shouting at me in the back of the ambulance as I writhed in pain. With anxiety, your mind creates perfectly imagined horror films constantly. It makes sense to you. It doesn't necessarily make sense to others, but it feels REAL.

Headache. A blinding tense one that you think is a brain tumor or meningitis. In fact, you don't THINK. You KNOW.

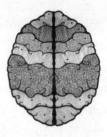

Like every atom in your body is about to explode. It itches. It BURNS. You read about spontaneous combustion. You are worried your body may catch fire.

Sweating. Not a glow. It pours off you like someone is holding a hose over your head. And not a nice garden hose, the high-pressure sort that tackles factory fires.

Nausea, stomach pain, diarrhea, vomiting. Perhaps all four at once. Yes, I've had all four at once.

With all this going on, it's no wonder that many anxiety sufferers feel scared or isolated. It's a very lonely condition. People can be very well-meaning, but you can sometimes be dismissed as weak, melodramatic, pathetic, or neurotic.

You're none of these things. You're an anxiety sufferer.

Anxiety is a prison that traps you everywhere. A prison that you can't escape from, and one not many people want to come and visit you in.

If you're nodding through any of this or you are identifying, I just want to give you a massive hug. It really is utterly shit. I've been there and I know. But it can, and it will, get better.

Let's look more at mechanisms for coping with anxiety. Mastering these can ease the feeling in the brain that something is terribly, terribly wrong.

Learn to Control the Physical Symptoms

Breathlessness can be scary, BUT it can ALSO be controlled.

Here's what I do. I should say now, this is JUST what I do. The good news is, there are lots of ways to tackle anxiety. Some people, with therapy, can "ride the wave" of their panic. Brain experts are finding new ways to tame brains constantly. This is just one example.

If I can, I lie on a bed or in the middle of an empty room. Failing that, I go and sit on a toilet. Then I breathe in for five seconds, hold it for seven seconds, and release it for ten seconds. I was taught this method by my school nurse Mrs. Kirby. She was terrifying but lovely to me—I think mainly because her dad had suffered with anxiety. She used to let me lie on the cot in her room until I felt better. Those fifteen-minute breaks helped me to pass multiple exams.

The Kirby Method™ still gets me through. I use it a lot, just because it works. As an aside, Mrs. Kirby passed away before I could thank her for this, so please make sure you tell people they are great before they die.

There are now also breathing apps to help you with this. (The presence of these should tell you how many of us lose control of our breathing on a daily basis.) Google a few methods, and find the one that suits you best. Deep breathing actually has a scientific basis behind it, because it activates the parasympathetic nervous system, which helps our bodies to relax.

If your stomach is affected by anxiety, peppermint capsules can really help with cramps. And smelling something strong can take the edge off the feeling of nervous nausea. I permanently have a well-known brand of menthol oil from Switzerland on a tissue to sniff.

If you're going somewhere, know where the toilets are so you don't have to rush. Putting little safety nets in place helps to take away the anxiety of being caught short or left high and dry.

I don't think my publishers thought I'd tackle bowel movements, but an increasing amount of research links bowel health and mental health. I told you we were going to be honest in this book. WE ARE TALKING NERVOUS POOP.

Make the Stuff That
Makes You Anxious Seem Silly

Make the scary things in your world absurd. Take your fears and make them small and silly. This works with phobias too. J. K. Rowling does this in the Harry Potter books when she makes Ron put spiders (which terrify him) on roller skates. It's a top idea. I made a graphic novel once called *Pepe the Rabid French Poodle*. Pepe had a mutant form of rabies that transformed him into a super dog who could save people. I realize rabies is not funny, but that little book is not going into print, and it helped me.

Whatever helps YOU (and doesn't hurt anyone else or yourself) is FINE.

My Anxiety Train and How
I Get Off at the Right Station

When my anxiety starts (usually in my gut), I visualize I'm on a train going down a track. That's what my anxiety feels like—fast. I can see what the destination is—a station in complete chaos. It's overcrowded, all the trains are late, the toilets have that "Closed for Cleaning" sign permanently in front of them and, worst of all, there's no café. It's everything terrible (but not too terrible) in one destination.

Then I imagine myself saying, "I'm not getting off there today."

I pull the emergency cord. The train jolts to a halt. The guard (who is the spitting image of my granddad) looks at me kindly. I explain to him that I need to get off because I'm having a massive panic attack. He says, "No worries, love. There's a lovely field over there with a Starbucks. Why don't you go and have a decaf latte? We'll wait and then we'll go back the other way. We shan't bother with the other place."

This is my fantasy. It doesn't have to make any sense or have any basis in reality.

Obviously you don't have to use this one. Not many people find trains as relaxing as I do. However, what you can do is explore your brain, find the comforting places of your mind, and practice going to them when you feel anxious. They can't be taken from you. They won't get torn down. They won't change unless you want them to. They are yours.

Your head doesn't have to be the thing that tortures you. It can be the place you go when you need to be happy and relaxed.

Learn from Your Experience

You only have to beat anxiety ONCE to know you can do it again and again. If you've left your house when you thought you couldn't ONCE, or have gone to a party you never thought you'd be able to ONCE, or visited the shops and looked a retail worker in the eye ONCE, THAT is a victory. That is a foundation to build on. Let all your little experiences of not being flattened by anxiety build and work for you.

Big statements in life rarely work ("I will be well and normal by tomorrow and everything will be FINE!") and often set you up for more anxiety if you don't manage to achieve them. Saying "I am doing the best I can and I am doing well. I am OK and these feelings will pass" as a substitute can serve to help anxiety pass more quickly. Small steps add up to HUGE things.

My experience has helped me. There is nothing I haven't been able to come back from—MAJOR passion with someone on a freezing golf course in November and being dumped two days later. Leaving one college after four days because I thought I was dying. Those are just two low points. There are many, many more. I came back from them all.

Not because I'm strong.

Just because I got back up again.

That's all you have to do.

For a lot of the time I was crawling, but I was, at least, moving.

Accept Failure

Failure is such a vital part of living well, but my anxiety came from a fear of it. We have to accept that failure will bite us all at some point. Don't be scared of it. It's the lion that you think is going to kill you. It looks terrifying. However, when it does catch you, it usually turns out to be a kitten that just mauls you a bit. You WILL find a way to wrestle out of its tiny paws.

That's another image I have in my head. I'm slightly cat obsessed.

In the end, we have to put ourselves out there. You've just got to do it. (Whatever "it" is.) Who cares if it doesn't work?! At least you've tried.

Overcoming your fear of failure is about letting your

mind take one step at a time. One word. One outing. One breath. If you break it down, it all seems much more achievable.

Other Things That Help

Even with the best coping mechanisms in the world, sometimes you need a bit of extra help to combat anxiety. Here are some of the options available—some work for me, some I'm not so keen on. The crucial thing with any mental health treatment is to find the balance and combination that works for you.

Psychotherapy

There are lots of different types of psychotherapy—your therapist will help you discover which one works best for you. I have had a lot of CBT, which stands for cognitive behavioral therapy, and I find it really effective in dealing with anxiety. It's used to treat many things, but it can help with anxiety by giving you ways to lose the feeling of being constantly on edge and scared.

Dr. R. says: *CBT looks at helping you to be more aware of your thoughts and feelings and how they affect your behavior. CBT aims to break the cycle of thoughts, feelings, and behavior to help reduce and manage anxiety.*

Mindfulness

Mindfulness has become a big thing in the past few years, and it's a skill REALLY worth having. (If you can, read Ruby Wax's book *A Mindfulness Guide for the Frazzled*. It's magnificent. There are also now mindfulness apps available.) However, it's worth saying that, for some people, practicing meditation or mindfulness can be a real leap at first. Quieting the brain can take a great deal of discipline. I find it REALLY hard.

Dr. R. says: *Mindfulness is based on the idea of becoming more aware of the present moment rather than racing into the future or dragging yourself back into the past with your thoughts.*

Distraction

A bored brain will create all sorts of trouble, and get anxious just because it can. You have to walk your mind like it's a border collie. Fill it with things you love. Get geeky. Get crafty. Memorize stuff. The more facts and passion and things you love that are in your mind, the less room there is for anxiety. At one stage, I could recite every number one song from 1952 onward thanks to *The Guinness Book of British Hit Singles*. Chart positions and song lyrics are still my party piece. When it comes to music, I was the internet before the internet.

Animals

If you love animals, there is something about being with them that just makes you feel more relaxed. They give far more than they take, and they don't demand too many complicated human qualities from you. Stroking a cat, feeding the birds, volunteering at an animal shelter, or looking after Roger, your sister's gerbil—it doesn't matter. Animals are great for anxiety. *(Note: If you are reading this in a rabies-affected country, just bear in mind that you shouldn't stroke animals you don't know. That's NOT an anxiety tip. That's a good piece of advice.)*

Nature

If you can, get out of the house and away from the city. Fields and forests and countryside can be incredibly calming. Especially with a magnificent playlist. To keep it safer, take someone with you, but make sure they've got their own headphones and music device. You can't be doing with idle chitchat when you have tunes and scenery.

Alternative Therapies

Some people find that therapies such as acupuncture, aromatherapy, and hypnotherapy really help them to deal with anxiety. Hypnotherapy is my favorite thing—I still go for a head tune-up like a car goes for a service. Hypnotherapists practice something called neuro-linguistic programming. Basically, they believe they can get to the back of your brain when you are in a relaxed state and straighten out the things that are causing problems. They have nothing to do with stage hypno-therapists and won't make you cluck like a chicken.

Dr. R. says: *The key thing with alterna-tive therapies is to find a practitioner you trust and know is reputable!*

Reality Champion

Get a Reality Champion. This isn't a "pull yourself together!" merchant. This is someone whom you can share your worst anxieties with and who can gently help you manage your worst thoughts if you are having an anxiety attack. My Reality Champion is my husband. You can use a friend, a partner, or a relative. It just has to be someone you trust.

Give them a worry and let them react rationally to it. Here are some of the things I've said to my partner over the years, and how he has reacted:

"I'm going to die."—Eventually. But not now.

"I've got cancer."—It's probably just irritable bowel syndrome. You've been checked.

"Everyone is going to hate my show. Hate it."—It's out there now. There's nothing you can do about it. Other people's opinions are not your business.

Reality Champions can help you to exercise that tiny part of your brain that isn't currently in the middle of the anxiety tsunami.

Medication

There are drugs available to help anxiety. But depending on the severity of your condition, your doctor may want to try other things first. There are a few reasons for this: We don't quite know the full effect of these drugs on growing brains, and they do come with side effects. They may make you sleepy for example or, alternatively, have insomnia.

In my case, on even a small dose of antianxiety medication, I can't write to the best of my ability. Normally words arrive easily in my head. But with medication it's like I'm reaching to grab language from the top shelf in a supermarket. I can eventually get there, but only after I've climbed on a few boxes.

Dr. R. says: *For some people in certain situations, medication can be useful, but it's important to talk with your doctor and develop a plan together, then to get more information about the medication available.*

Stress (and How to Punch It in the Face)

Anxiety and stress are roommates. They live together in their apartment, screaming and throwing plates at each other. So it's no surprise that they share many of the same symptoms.

All of us will have stress in our lives because life is stressful. That is possibly the most obvious statement I've ever written, but it's true. On top of all the stuff happening in our personal lives, the world has a certain number of total idiots in it. Many of these idiots have managed to get into positions of power. Yes, you know who I'm talking about. However, there have ALWAYS been idiots, and there always will be. Likewise, there will always be demands on you. Frankly, there are some days when I find doing the washing stressful. It's the whole sorting-out-the-whites-from-the-red-stuff thing. *(It has been hard to move on from a time in 1992 when I ruined a Smiths T-shirt by turning it pink. Not even my mom could save it, and she did laundry professionally in a boarding school for years. What she doesn't know about a hot wash isn't worth knowing.)*

It can genuinely be hard to move on from these moments and trust yourself again. Stress grows from doubt like a weed. It strangles your confidence and makes you feel like you're not in control.

Stress can make your heart race, your mouth dry, and your stomach feel like a washing machine on a fast, panicked spin (yes—like the one the Smiths T-shirt was on). You have no tolerance or patience for the people around you. You snap at nice questions like "Would you like a cup of tea and a cookie?" and you can't sleep. Life seems like a mountain range of problems you can't get across. The Himalayas of Complete Ass. You manage to get to the summit of one problem, and another one magically appears. It looms in the distance—something else you have to scale on top of all the other nonsense.

The trick is to try to make your mountains into molehills. They're annoying, but you can step over them.

STRESS IS DEBILITATING AND CAN BE SCARY, BUT IT CAN ALSO BE OVERCOME.

Here are some ideas on how to cope with stress:

REMEMBER, SO LITTLE IN LIFE ACTUALLY MATTERS.

This sounds depressing. It isn't. It's a way of releasing you from all the small stuff.

Sometimes we all get stressed about things we can do nothing about, and about things that don't really matter.

I remember once having a frankly pathetic tantrum about the lack of vegetarian sandwiches at my favorite lunch spot. From the start of the day, I'd had my heart set on a precise lunch plan. My day was built around it. Then I went down there and it looked like there'd been a chilled cabinet decimation. My sandwich was gone. My true love had been taken. That was IT! I wasn't having anything! I WAS GOING TO GO HUNGRY. I stormed back to my desk and shouted at my friend Dave, "THEY WERE OUT OF WENSLEYDALE AND CARROT. CAN YOU EVEN BELIEVE IT?!"

I then put a can of soda through my keyboard in a temper. To be fair, the lack of appropriate lunch options wasn't the real problem. I was stressed about the fact I'd had a pap smear and it had come back inconclusive. Consequently, every tiny disappointment turned into a disaster.

Vocalizing this to a guy dressed in a Sunderland

soccer shirt, chowing down on half a cow, may not have been helpful, but Dave offered a super and simple bit of advice. It's a life philosophy I've carried with me ever since.

Looking up from his screen, Dave calmly said, "You could have just had Brie and grape."

He was right, of course. I could.

Two vital lessons were learned here. I'd added silly stress to my real stress by getting obsessed about a tiny thing (the right type of cheese) and not tackling what was really stressing me out (my health).

It's not the end of the world if you don't get exactly what you want or things don't run exactly on time. In a hundred years, will the history books record the day my sandwich wasn't available? No. A day after, did it matter? No. The next time you're stressing over something, ask yourself (a) is Brie and grape available? And (b) what's the REAL problem?

Real, legitimate, stress-causing problems are another matter, but they are also rarely the end of the world.

Relationships may end, but you will have other relationships. At times, it can feel like we'll be single forever, but we won't—unless we want to be. Friendships may explode in arguments and anger, but they can be mended, or you can meet other lovely people. Exams may be failed, but they can be retaken. We can all (and I TOTALLY include myself in this) sometimes put too much emphasis on too many things. If you're feeling stressed about your education, remember that many people have spectacularly failed exams (me) and still managed to have a successful career (also me).

I'm not saying "Don't care about anything," though. Quite the opposite. One thing that ALWAYS matters is your health—both physical and mental. You need to look after that, so you need to learn to manage stress.

All great achievements usually involve struggle, setbacks, and pain. That's why life is so often referred to as a marathon, not a sprint. Having done the London Marathon, and openly sobbed from mile fourteen to mile twenty-two, I can tell you this really is true. However, the lost toenails and the inability to walk the next day were ALL worth it for that medal. I'd done it. I'd conquered my demons and the people who said that I'd never be able to do it. Yes, I was overtaken by a camel, a golfer, a Dalek, and an entire battalion of the army carrying a two-ton cannon, but I finished. I took it one step, and one stress, at a time. THAT is the way to finish anything, SO here are some steps to help you conquer stress:

Buffer Your Life

I really want to slap my phone when it buffers an HD movie, but actually it's setting a fantastic life example. If everything feels like it's too much, choose not to download it all at once. Find out the most important thing you have to do and focus on completing that task. Buffer everything else. It can wait.

Social Media

Take yourself off social media for a set period every day. It's HARD. I find it hard, but we are not designed to be constantly connected to other humans. No, I'm not suggesting you give up Twitter, Snapchat, Instagram, or any other social media platform. I couldn't cope with that either. It's just for a time every day, to help you clear your head of all the noise.

Air-Traffic-Control Your Existence

Sorry, we are back to planes again. It's just that air traffic controllers are the masters of both organization and controlling stress. I crush hard on them for this. In the old days, they used to manage their airspace by stacking the planes up one by one on little "strips" (metal bars with the name of the plane on each one).

When each plane was dealt with, they got rid of the strip. I still use this system. Write down each thing you have to do on a piece of paper and, once you've completed it, throw it away. It's very satisfying and easy to keep track of.

Air traffic controllers also only work for forty-five minutes at a time, and then they take fifteen minutes off. Time out controls stress and improves concentration. FACT.

I now PROMISE I won't mention planes again.*

*I can't promise this.

Stones

Put your worries on a stone and throw that stone in a pond, a river, or the sea. A puddle will do. Seeing your worries disappear in water feels like you are drowning your stress.

Put Your Stresses in the Grocery Store Parking Lot

This technique is very handy at night. When I feel like I have a lot to contend with, I imagine that my stresses are vehicles. I visualize the grocery store parking lot in Stamford, where I grew up. I stand outside the shop. First, I put some wonderful things I have to do/people I have to see in the spots nearest the entrance. I make them HUGE 4x4 Range Rovers.

Then I start filling up the rest of the parking lot with everything else in my head. Row by row. Things I have to deal with, things I cannot control, and, far away, in the corner by the car wash, the horrible things that can NEVER be made better but I have to live with. By making those problems bad cars like Reliant Robins (google them if you are not familiar) and parking them out of sight, I acknowledge them, but I take them out of my vision AND take their power away. Life is not neat, and sometimes we need smart ways to make it tidier.

What to Do When World Events Seem Dreadful and Stressful

Not very long ago, the only sources of "news" were newspapers, scheduled news bulletins on TV and the radio, and your friends and neighbors. This has obviously now changed.

There is no doubt in my mind that had the term "snowflake" existed in my youth it would have been used against me. I couldn't cope with anything. However, saying you can't cope with an endless stream of media focusing on death and destruction doesn't make you a snowflake. It makes you sensible.

When world events seem like they are too much to take in, turn social media or rolling news coverage off. This does not mean you don't care. It means you are making the conscious and responsible decision to remove yourself from a situation you currently cannot help with. When you are ready to catch up with what is happening, use a reputable news source. I always suggest the BBC—NO, I DO NOT WORK FOR THEM—because I know that their facts have to be checked and they are obliged to show both sides of an argument. The news will be presented to you in a non-sensationalized way with an emphasis on what has happened, rather than speculation or hysteria.

Unless you are a world leader or in the media, no one is waiting for your reaction to any global event. Release yourself from that responsibility—it doesn't actually exist.

Useful Stress and When It's OK to Panic

I'm not stupid or ignorant. Consequently I don't like being treated as though I am. I imagine you are exactly the same.

You'll know that inevitably you are going to find yourself in challenging situations. You may even find yourself in situations that feel scary or intimidating.

This is where stress actually does a really important job, and why it's in all of us.

You'll know if you are caught in a really dangerous situation. It will feel different. And it may surprise you how you respond.

If you've suffered from anxiety or stress, you are better practiced and built for real crisis. You may find that people who are everyday towers of strength crumble in the wake of something extraordinary, but your adrenaline is already primed.

Your brain may astound you. There is no real way to predict how brains are going to react. Some very ordinary and tortured people have done some extraordinary things under extreme conditions.

A fit and trained brain can do hard stuff like a fit body can do a marathon. In fact, a fit brain got me through the London Marathon. My legs didn't. I'd only been training for three months.

The anxious brain won't fold in a crisis. It's prepared for it. So there is no reason why you should feel less about yourself if you are an anxiety or stress sufferer. That's nonsense. You've already survived the countless stresses of your own head. You're more ready than you'll ever know for lots of things. You're ready for life.

"IT'S A LABURNUM TREE!!! GET AWAY FROM IT!!"

Phobias

I think phobias are a very intelligent and rather sophisticated offshoot of anxiety. I would say that because I've had a few, but I do think they are a product of the brain being very clever. It tries to fix all your terror, stress, and anxiety by focusing on one thing—sensible, when you think about it. Rather than being terrified of everything, your mind decides it's frightened of very specific things and you only have to avoid those to be completely safe.

Here are some of the things I've been phobic of in my life:

BUTTON BATTERIES

BLEACH

GERMS

BERRIES

WATER

THE ENTIRE AMANITA FUNGI FAMILY
(Including the death cap and the
destroying angel)

RABIES
(We've covered that)

NEEDLES
(The sewing variety)

VOMIT

YEW TREES
(The seed inside the berry is deadly, but the
red flesh outside isn't)

LABURNUM TREES
(A common tree with yellow blossoms and
very poisonous, pea-pod-style seeds)

Later in the chapter, I'm going to use laburnum trees as an example of what a phobia feels like and how it can affect your life. In my case it was quite dramatically. My life stopped because of a tree. Yes, you can laugh at that. It's fine to laugh now. It wasn't at the time. Phobias can be very funny but also very sad. Some people suffer with turophobia. That's the fear of cheese. What a genuinely terrible thing to suffer with—I mean that.

Anyway. What's the difference between a phobia and a fear? You know what a fear, or "fear," usually feels like. It shares a lot of symptoms with anxiety. Your heart beats incredibly fast, you feel nervous and sick, you have a tingly feeling in your entire body, and you can't shift your mind away from what is making you scared.

Fear is usually a direct response to something it's understandable to be frightened of. It's OK to be frightened of new situations. It's right to be scared of someone holding a gun and threatening to shoot you. It's right to be full of fear about an exam that you think your whole life rests on. (It doesn't, by the way, but I can understand why you think it might. I did the same.)

All of those things make sense. The fear makes sense.

A phobia is something different. It's fear on steroids.

Phobias are huge. They compromise every part of your life. The fear of the (often harmless or controllable) thing you are phobic of takes over, and you build your life around managing and avoiding the fear.

Sometimes phobias have a cause that's easy to understand. Things that happen in early childhood can lead to phobias. If you have a bad experience with something, your brain can make a HUGE DANGER bookmark to keep you safe. Your mind here is trying to do a good thing. It's just made the size of the fear wrong, but your phobia

may come from a very obvious and legitimate place. For much of my life, I was terrified of water, for a very good reason. As a kid, I nearly drowned in Spain when my spotted *101 Dalmatians* inflatable ring decided to deflate. I can remember sinking to the bottom of the swimming pool and watching all the feet kick above me. My brother fished me out. I did eventually learn to swim, but I haven't been in a pool since 2001.

However, some phobias cannot be traced back to anything specific and are probably part of a more general feeling of deep anxiety.

Let's use my laburnum tree example.

I was so frightened of laburnum trees that I made a mental map of every one of them in my hometown so I could avoid them. There used to be a huge one on Waverley Gardens, which was full of fancy houses and Laburnum Central. Unfortunately, it was also the quickest route to my brother's house. So instead of going on a twenty-minute walk there, I went on a forty-five-minute one just to avoid the laburnum hell. This often involved going past a huge cemetery at night. But a meeting with a member of the undead was preferable to walking under a laburnum tree.

If I ever did have to walk under one, I would clamp my mouth together until my lips were sore and then spit into my hand after I'd passed it just to check no pods had flown in. Writing this now it seems ridiculous, but I know I did it for YEARS. I'd certainly never talk under a laburnum tree. If a friend asked me something, I'd go mute or pretend I had a five-second sore throat, or that I just hadn't heard and make a quizzical face. It's very difficult to have a conversation when you're worried about being accidentally killed by a breeze full of poisonous pods.

Don't feel bad if you're thinking, "She's weird." Phobias ARE weird. Some people are scared of zippers. How can you be phobic of zippers? They are a magnificently useful invention, they make a lovely noise, and they earn you shedloads of points in Scrabble.

But none of that matters if you are scared of them. It doesn't matter what they are to everyone else. To you they are the worst thing on earth. That terror is real, and the fear it creates is crippling. It has the same effect as a shark standing in front of you with a knife and fork saying they'd quite fancy a human for dinner. It's an immediate and COMPLETE BODY RED ALERT situation. You need to escape, get away, and never be near a zip again.

In my case (not all phobias are about this), what I was really frightened of was dying, and the trouble with death is that it's eventually going to happen to all of us. I didn't get my head around that for years, and this fear of dying, this fear of not being on this earth and leaving the people I loved in a terrible state of grief, made me phobic of just about everything that could hurt me. I lived with it until one day when I decided . . .

What did I decide? I think I was just exhausted with fear and sick of being afraid. Perhaps I didn't care anymore. Or I felt brave that day. Anyway, I walked under a laburnum tree with my mouth slightly ajar.

Nothing flew in.

The next time I walked under the tree with my mouth wide open. Nothing flew in.

(Although the woman walking toward me thought I was really odd.)

Now I can walk under laburnum trees normally. I just don't want one in a sandwich. Thank you.

Gently testing yourself is a good thing to do with phobias. It can take A LONG TIME to build up the strength to do this, but, as with many mental health conditions, small steps can make ALL the difference. Walking under a tree with my mouth open may not seem particularly courageous. However, if you've had a phobia, you'll know it took a lot of psyching up and positive self-encouragement to tackle these things. "Come on, Rae. You CAN do this. You've just been to Peterborough on a day trip! YOU CAN TAKE ON THE TREE!"

The stupid thing is, I was too embarrassed to tell the medical professionals that could have helped me with my phobias. I opted for a life of clamped mouths, sore lips, constant tree terror, and huge long walks past newly dug graves. My way of coping cost me so much time and mental effort. I will keep repeating this—however stupid or terrible you think the thing you are thinking is, TALK TO YOUR DOCTOR. THEY CAN HELP. YOU DESERVE BETTER THAN THIS.

Your doctor can talk you through all the alternative ways to deal with your phobia. These can include:

Psychotherapy

Cognitive Behavioral Therapy, or CBT, is a type of psychotherapy that can help most people overcome or better manage their phobia. Counseling can also be a helpful form of psychotherapy for phobias. You can talk through your phobia and the things that may have caused it in a safe environment. If it's a phobia that appeared from nowhere, your doctor can help you to manage the anxiety and give you ways to tackle both your phobia and the behaviors that result from it.

Exposure Therapy

You talk through your fear as you are gradually exposed to the thing you are scared of. For example, if you are frightened of spiders a therapist will show you images and videos of them. They may take you to a place where you expect to see a spider (for example, a bathroom or barn). Eventually you may sit in a room with an actual spider in a covered tank. This will then be uncovered so you can look at the spider. Then the therapist will move the tank closer and closer to you. This will all be done in a very gentle, controlled way—no horrible shocks or surprises. It's gradual and done at your own speed. I suppose walking under the tree with my mouth open was a bit of amateur exposure therapy. Although ideally, exposure therapy shouldn't take eleven years to work.

By the end of one session, some people can actually hold the thing they are scared of. This sort of therapy is often combined with . . .

Hypnotherapy

A hypnotherapist I know used to run an arachnophobia (fear of spiders) course at a zoo, and he told me something really interesting. Sometimes when people didn't respond well to phobia treatment, it was because their phobia was "working" for them in another way. Perhaps it was keeping them safe from something else. Isn't the brain incredible? It's worth remembering that sometimes when we think it's working against us, it's actually working for us.

> **Dr. R. says:** *Certain phobias may have origi-nated in something that, at some stage of human evolution, kept us safe. However, when a phobia is taken to an extreme or when it is limiting our daily lives, we need to seek support in overcoming it.*

Social Phobia, or Social Anxiety Disorder

Lots of us can really empathize with social phobia. The fear of meeting, speaking, or interacting with others can cause us a great deal of stress. At its most extreme, social phobia can strip you of the pleasure of being with people and feeling comfortable with other human beings. It can have you begging for the zombie apocalypse to happen just so you don't have to face FACES.

Social phobia can reduce your confidence or convince you that you are worth nothing to other people, and nothing you say could be interesting to them. You feel boring and dull before you open your mouth. You may have a heightened sense that everyone is looking at you. My social phobia didn't lead to silence and withdrawal—it led to verbal diarrhea. We shouldn't always assume that quiet people have social phobia and loud ones don't. Fear and terror of others comes in all shapes, noises, and sizes.

You may feel that if you do go out and meet people,

they will judge or criticize you. If I ever had to eat in front of anyone else, I was sure I could hear them whispering, "She's disgusting!" and "Listen to the noise." Every movement I made, and every chew and swallow, seemed to be attracting scientific levels of scrutiny. It's like EVERYONE is looking at you and talking about YOU all of the time. And it's not good talk either. This can lead to physical symptoms such as your heart beating really fast, or you may blush red, start sweating, or feel faint.

All mental health problems can make you feel isolated, but this one can be really cruel because the help you need comes from other human beings, and that's precisely what you FEAR.

It's worth making the distinction here between social anxiety and being an introvert. Being an introvert does NOT need a cure. The world needs introverts. There's nothing wrong with being the sort of person who doesn't like big groups and prefers one-on-one company.

I also HATE the word shy. What IS shy? My husband is an introvert and was constantly accused of being "shy" as a child. In the end, he said it was a label that made him feel incredibly self-conscious. That word is now banned in our house because it's so often used to bully people who are just a little bit more cautious about forming relationships with others or who carefully consider what they are going to say. There is nothing wrong with wanting to speak less than other people, and to build intimate relationships more gradually. That is NOT a social phobia. That is a personality type that the world NEEDS.

There are plenty of ways to live a magnificent life.

The world needs ALL sorts of people doing all sorts of things. If you're an introvert who is comfortable and happy to be introverted, THAT IS FINE.

Don't be told it's all about making LOTS of friends, going to all the parties and bungee jumping naked off bridges in New Zealand. It might be for you. But it might also be gardening. Or jigsaw puzzles. Or knitting. Or, in fact, all of those things. It might be reading for hours or re-creating dance moves in your front room. (Yes—I still do that today.) WHO CARES? Do what you like. There is no such thing as a guilty pleasure. There is just PLEASURE.

The world needs ALL sorts of people doing all sorts of things. If you're an introvert who is comfortable and happy to be introverted, THAT IS FINE.

If you do suffer from social phobia, however, there are a few things you can do to ease any situation. If you have a few basic social survival strategies, you can get through quite a lot.

Try to Get Out There a Bit

The first step is ALWAYS the hardest, but (as approximately eight billion memes will tell you) even the biggest journey starts with one small step. Go to a library. People are there for a specific purpose, and you can be among them in the quiet. Off-peak public transportation is good for this too. In both situations, you'll need to have some interaction, but it can be controlled and limited. It's a good way to dip your toe in the water.

Confront Your Worst Fears

Write down all the terrible things you think people think about you. I will write some of mine here:

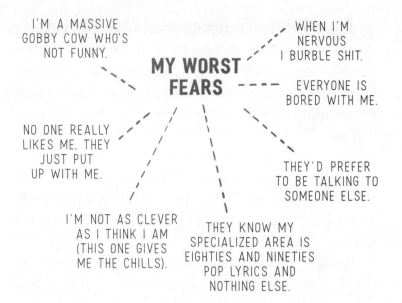

MY WORST FEARS

I'M A MASSIVE GOBBY COW WHO'S NOT FUNNY.

WHEN I'M NERVOUS I BURBLE SHIT.

EVERYONE IS BORED WITH ME.

NO ONE REALLY LIKES ME, THEY JUST PUT UP WITH ME.

THEY'D PREFER TO BE TALKING TO SOMEONE ELSE.

I'M NOT AS CLEVER AS I THINK I AM (THIS ONE GIVES ME THE CHILLS).

THEY KNOW MY SPECIALIZED AREA IS EIGHTIES AND NINETIES POP LYRICS AND NOTHING ELSE.

Then, next to each question, answer it with THIS TOTAL TRUTH:

WHAT OTHER PEOPLE THINK OF ME IS NOT MY BUSINESS. I HAVE NO CONTROL OVER IT. I'M AS GOOD AS THE NEXT PERSON. I HAVE SOMETHING TO OFFER.

There are stronger, more empowering, versions of this, but this is the one I can truthfully own. Every time that critic starts barking in your head, SHOUT it down with that.

Do a MILITARY Reconnaissance Mission

When I was growing up, I lived near a US Air Force base. A huge, scary American intelligence-gathering plane called an AWACS used to fly over my house. It had a massive rotating radar on the back.

Oh.

Sorry, we're on planes again.

Look. It's a great example of something I want to talk about, so live with it. Taking care of your head sometimes means changing the rules, so the no-plane rule is off for the time being.

Anyway, before I do anything new or go anywhere different (place, party, interview, shop), I do a RAEWACS mission. It REALLY helps.

If you know you're going somewhere new and you're worried about it, do a reconnaissance run. Go and look at where you are going and find out what the place is like. OR google it. Use Google Maps with Street View. If you can plan your route and look at the building and street you are going to, it's FAR less stressful.

Turn Bad Brain Off.
Turn Observation Brain On.

Make your brain concentrate on what YOU think about things, NOT on what people might think about YOU.

When you're out and about, turn the volume down on your internal "bad" voice and turn the volume up on your observational skills. Look at where you are. What does the place look like? What does it smell like? Why does that elevator not have a level thirteen? If you're in someone's house, look at their decor. What's the flooring like? What decorations do they have? Was that big flower-print wallpaper a smart choice? If you concentrate on everything going on around you, then you spend less time thinking about what other people may or may not think of you.

Find a Tribe

This sounds terrifying. But all I'm really suggesting you do is find a few people that are like you. Look around. It's fairly easy to spot people who aren't exactly loving the situation. For lots of us, social situations are not the easiest thing. Look in the corners of the room. Is there someone on their own? As you observe your surroundings, take a look at the people there too.

Ask People About Themselves

One of life's great secrets is that most people absolutely love talking about themselves. At length. And many of them do not feel the need to ask you about yourself in return. Let them talk. It takes ALL the pressure off you.

I'm good at asking strangers questions, and because of this I know some amazing things, like how Tesco stores in Essex get their deliveries, which celebrities are nice in real life, and what it's like to be in a war.

Good general subjects to talk about are music, celebrities, books, films, vacations, and education. Ask questions. People will LOVE you for it. Also, find out their name and use it all the time. The more you use it, the more they'll love you. Seriously. It's in the small details. We all like to feel important.

You could try politics, but that can go bad very quickly. Some people don't know how to argue properly.

Remember Other Humans Are Just Human

Authority can be scary. A really good thing to do with people in power is to make them all VERY human. I have a well-established and frankly brilliant way of handling scary people. It's slightly vile, but it works. I just imagine them on the toilet.

No one is scary on the toilet and everyone has to use it.

If someone is bullying or intimidating you, being overbearing, and increasing your social anxiety, just imagine them in bad underpants in the bathroom. If you reduce powerful human beings to what they are (just humans), it makes everything easier to cope with.

And Here's a Massive Secret That Sounds Pretty Dreadful But It's Not . . .

Somebody once said to me, "So little in this world is really about you."

This made me feel incredibly sad, but it's actually not, if you think about it. You spend more time thinking about yourself and your feelings than you do about others. This isn't selfishness. It's just how we are. It's how we look after ourselves. Even with social anxiety, you are still thinking about what people think of YOU. You are still thinking of you. I'm not saying there is anything wrong with this—I'm just saying that's how most of us are.

Just release yourself from the center of things. You

ARE important to the people who love you. You're important to this world. You don't know yet what YOU are going to achieve (that applies to you whatever age you are). However, the world does not pivot on you. Thank GOD.

When you release yourself from being the center of things, you also release yourself from worrying too much about what everyone thinks.

When People Do Have a Bad or Nasty Reaction to You, Remember It's About Them, Not You

People's reaction to you often has much more to do with them, and how they are feeling, than it does with you. If someone is abrupt, unkind, or rude to you, it's probably because they're having a bad day, or because they're not a very nice person. It's not really anything to do with you at all. So LEAVE it with them. Leave all their awful words with them. Leave all the awful feelings it produces with them. Their opinion means nothing.

People's reaction to you is a reflection of where they are. Perhaps they are sad or angry. Perhaps they just want to feel powerful by making someone else feel lousy. Perhaps they've been reading comments from trolls and they want to snap at someone. You can spend ages trying to work out the motivation as to why someone said or did something. But you'll be torturing yourself needlessly, as you will never truly know. Perhaps even THEY will never truly know.

"IT'S JUST FOOD BUT IT'S <u>NOT</u> JUST FOOD!"

Eating Disorders

There are many types of eating disorders, and sadly, they are very common. There are very good reasons for this.

Even before our brains have started thinking about it, people are trying to affect how we feel about our bodies every day. Sometimes it's because they want to improve our physical health (the medical profession), sometimes it's because they want to sell us something (the diet and beauty industry), and sometimes it's because they want to make us feel lousy (trolls).

They've been doing it for years too. Do this diet. Do that diet. Don't eat fat. Eat fat. Be skinny. No! Be curvy. Actually be skinny and curvy. Beat the bloat! Here's my avocado salad on rye bread. Look at me chomping on this hamburger, yet I'm a size zero. Eat something skinny. Don't be skinny, though. Or do be skinny. Don't eat something fatty.

OH, EAT WHAT YOU BLOODY LIKE AND LOOK HOW YOU BLOODY LIKE!

But that's easier said than done. I KNOW.

Also, and I'm going to be honest with you, I think the relationship we have with food and body image may have gotten even harder to manage in recent years. I love social media, but it's had a really detrimental effect on how we see both food and ourselves. Everything on social media is perfectly posed. Cheesecakes in the Lo-Fi filter, selfies taken a billion times to get the best one. (WE ALL DO THIS. MY MOM DOES IT. SHE IS SEVENTY-FOUR.) Everywhere, there are beauty secrets, contouring, clean eating (what is dirty eating?! OH, DO GET LOST!), sculpturing, eye perfecting . . . I'm EXHAUSTED. Even writing that makes me tired. I can't do all that. I can't BE all that. Does that make me less? Should I do all that more? Would I be more if there was less of me?

NO.

Let me tell you what I have to remind myself every day:

You are enough.

YOU ARE ENOUGH.

YOU ARE ENOUGH.

This is how some eating disorders start. There is so much noise coming from all directions that we start to doubt ourselves, and our looks. We begin to think we are not enough, we are somehow wrong, and there's a "right" that we should be aiming for.

There is no right. There's no perfection. But the way we feel about food can be affected by the belief that there is. There isn't. I promise.

However, eating disorders are complicated. We can't just blame them on traditional or social media. There is pressure on us to look good and to fit into the beauty stereotypes that we see everywhere. But food is also a very accessible thing to control or abuse. We have to have food. It's not like a problem with alcohol or drugs, where you can cut them out of your life completely. We can't avoid food. We need it. I think this is why eating disorders are so widespread.

Many of us suffer at one time or another, and sometimes it can be a lifelong battle.

In my teens, I was a chronic overeater. I ate to excess to forget and to comfort the parts of me that were raging. All the pain inside me could be temporarily soothed with chips dipped in Philadelphia cream cheese. I could stave off my anxiety with loads of cookies. The junk food sang to me like a chorus. "Come to us in the cupboard. We love you, Rae. We demand nothing. Just undress us. Eat us."

You probably know about that by now, but what you don't know is what happened after I decided to lose the excess weight comfort eating had created. I had a very fixed set of ideas about what life would be like when I was thin.

What Will Certainly Happen When I Am Thin
By Rae, age 16

I will be happy. I will have a glow about me every morning. A golden glow of the freshest beauty.

I will be in a great relationship. My partner will love and treasure me. My body, brain, and tremendous wit will be adored. I will wake up every morning with his big manly arms around my waist. MY WAIST. I WILL HAVE A WAIST.

I will look really sexy in men's shirts and even sports bras. My lingerie drawer will be a perfectly calm and ordered ocean of silky lacy things floating around. In fact, I will be floating, tiny underwear and all.

I will be really into myself. Every look in the mirror will be a journey of total self-love. I will have to masturbate immediately as soon as I look at myself.

I will NEVER feel bad again. I will be ALL-POWERFUL. My weight will change everything. I know, with total certainty, that life will change completely if I CAN JUST BE THIN. My MAGIC weight will make my life spectacular. No. It REALLY will.

I'm five foot four, and I weighed 203 pounds when I started dieting.

Every time I felt like comfort eating, I would imagine one of the boys who called me Jabba gasping with lust as I drifted by them. And their face of pain as I sensationally rejected them—often by saying, "Remember me? Don't recognize ME, do you?" My long hair would blow in the wind like Wonder Woman's. I was SENSATIONAL. My revenge fantasies would go on for HOURS. DAYS. I would also look in the mirror and tell myself I didn't deserve anything nice because I was FAT and UGLY and USELESS.

This was especially stupid because your brain records everything you do and believes everything you say. If you're talking to yourself like that, it is WRONG. Please stop immediately. I didn't for years, and it took a long time to convince my brain otherwise.

I eventually reached 124 pounds. I was weighing myself at the pharmacy every other day; the machine printed off your receipts. I kept them and made a caterpillar of sensational pound loss. And as the weight fell off, something amazing happened:

Nothing.

Don't get me wrong. For two weeks in the nineties, I was wearing tiny Topshop velvet hot pants. My body changed. No surprise. I was monitoring calories like a sparrow hawk eyes up pigeons. READY TO ATTACK anything fatty and destroy it by clawing it into the trash.

Every day followed the same routine. It was ALL about the food. A carefully measured bowl of cereal with skim milk for breakfast. A huge hunger crawl to lunch. A tiny baked potato with nothing on it but a can of tinned tomatoes. Finally, for dinner, a small plate of pasta with ANOTHER tin of tomatoes. Then a yogurt. The yogurt was the highlight of my day.

That's no way to live. I was miserable. I'd go past Pizza Hut with my mouth closed just in case the smell of the place had any calories. And yes, that does sound like my laburnum phobia, doesn't it? Can you see a pattern forming here?

There was no self-love, no longing looks in the mirror, my underwear drawer had one G-string that I still didn't feel good in, and I still hated anyone touching me.

In short, I still felt dreadful. Nothing had changed. My head stayed in exactly the same place it had been at 203 pounds.

And that's because . . .

Feeling truly good doesn't come from a number on a scale. Magic weights do not exist.

An unhealthy relationship with food can display itself in lots of ways.

How Do You Know You Have an Eating Disorder?

You are severely restricting your calorie intake (anorexia).

You are making yourself sick after eating (bulimia).

You think about food obsessively.

You are frightened about consuming accidental calories and weigh yourself often. Perhaps you weigh yourself several times a day. If your weight increases by even a tiny amount, you are distressed.

You binge on food. You may or may not make yourself sick after this. It happens particularly when you are feeling sad, angry, lonely, or emotional. You eat constantly, even when you are not hungry. The prospect of having to deal with food makes you anxious or unhappy.

You may avoid going out with friends or family if food is involved, and become socially isolated.

Though anorexia and binge eating seem like direct opposites of each other, I think all eating disorders have one thing in common. They are, bizarrely, not really about food. They're about the other stuff going on in our heads. Just like the title of this chapter suggests, this isn't just about food and how we see ourselves. They're a symptom of bigger emotional issues. For example, many of us fear we have no control, so we control our food intake. I binged to cope with my anxiety. Sometimes that's harder to work out than restricting calories or eating ten chocolate cookies or making ourselves sick.

Perhaps you're unhappy at school, or you've lost control in a certain situation and are trying, via food, to get it back. Having a family history of eating disorders is a risk factor in developing one yourself. And there's also growing evidence that some eating disorders may even be genetic.

To recover from any eating disorder, you are going to need professional help. I did. And once I got it, I was able to work out what the REAL problems were. This enabled me to build my self-esteem (see the self-esteem chapter for tips) and to REALLY enjoy my life—regardless of my size. And my weight fluctuates. I don't look in the mirror most days and think, "YOU SEXUAL GODDESS," but even on my worst days I do think, "Yeah. I'll do. That's fine."

That's self-acceptance. That is an essential thing you need to grow and work on for EVERY aspect of your mental health.

Not treating anorexia and bulimia appropriately can also lead to a whole host of very real medical emergencies and long-term health problems. I'm not trying to alarm or frighten you, but I don't want to lie to you either. Likewise, binge eating can, in the long term, cause far-reaching health issues. I know from my own experience that, at the time, I didn't give a toss about long-term health effects, and it's very difficult not to turn this into a tedious nag/guilt session. Sorry. I feel like I am lecturing you. I'm not. It's just I know eating disorders can go on in secret for so long. I've done, or I know people who have done, the things that hide the problems. Wearing baggy clothes to hide weight loss, pretending you're ill to avoid food, using mouthwash to hide the smell of vomit, creating a graveyard of chocolate wrappers behind your bed because you're eating so much. And I want you to realize that these things can have long-term repercussions for your health. If you're doing any of them, PLEASE talk to someone.

In the Meantime, Here Are a Few Things That Can Help:

Try to retrace your mental steps. When did your eating disorder start? This can help to uncover what it is really about.

Ask yourself—What is this behavior with food doing for me? How does it make me feel? When I'm eating, how do I feel? When I'm not eating, how do I feel? When I'm purging, how do I feel?

Write down the feelings you have associated with food. What's it doing for you? Misusing food may be serving a purpose for you—my binge eating was helping me cope with my anxiety.

Get yourself off pro-ana sites. NOW. How do I know about these? Because occasionally a Google alert tells me I've been mentioned on one. I looked at a pro-ana site, and I was horrified by what I read there. There is a vast difference between a supportive online community and people making each other more ill by sharing extreme slimming tips. Leave. Get off. Do it today.

Take one day at a time. Things that happen are just moments. If they go wrong, let them pass. I'm going to say it again:

GIVE YOURSELF A BREAK.

The first and most important step in getting better is to tell someone you trust and who loves you, such as a family member. They can support you in seeking help from a doctor.

Eating disorders can get better with the right help. Depending on your specific case, your doctor may refer you to a team of specialists including a CBT therapist, a nutritionist, or a psychotherapist who uses a different type of talking therapy. They are all there to support you and help you in all aspects of your eating disorder, to help you feel well again.

Sometimes family therapy is useful too, and some people use medication to help their recovery. You can be given these treatments as an outpatient (which means you go into a hospital or other center regularly to see people) or sometimes in a residential center, which will give you more intensive support.

Your friends and family are also a key part of recovery

to keep you steady, so use them as much as possible! Never be afraid to ask questions. No question is stupid. "What color are the sofas in the ward where I will be staying?" is a perfectly acceptable question. I have asked this, and it was answered (blue).

You and your body deserve to be nourished, not punished by deprivation or excess. You deserve more. You deserve to have a relationship with food that doesn't dominate your life. And if you're currently telling me you don't—you're wrong. I'm right. Please repeat NOW sixty times, "I've just been speaking to Rae and she thinks I deserve more. She is totally correct."

I'm just helping your brain tell the truth.

"IF I JUST SAY THE WORD 'GOD' TWELVE TIMES, MY MOM WON'T DIE IN THE BUS SHE'S TRAVELING TO WORK ON"

 OCD

As I'm a known sufferer of OCD, some people are very disappointed when they visit my house. They are expecting a palace of cleanliness and hygiene—instead they come into an asthmatic's nightmare. There are dust balls that can be easily modeled into small animals. (In fact, I've done this activity with my son—hours of cheap fun!) These dust balls roll around my wood floors like tumbleweed in the desert. There are spiderwebs on the ceiling (I currently live in Australia; they are BIG webs) and soap scum on the taps. My ornaments are all over the place, and when I get the vacuum cleaner out, my son thinks it feels like a special occasion.

Some people think I'm too untidy to have obsessive compulsive disorder. This is because the term OCD has become a lazy way of saying you're really tidy, or you like things to be in a certain order.

An obsession with hygiene and extreme cleanliness can absolutely be a symptom of OCD. I'll talk more about that later. However, obsessive compulsive disorder is actually about all sorts of recurrent and intrusive thoughts that give you a compulsion to DO something or to repeat a pattern of behaviors over and over and over again. These behaviors lessen your anxiety slightly, but this is ONLY temporary and in the long term your general anxiety builds and your compulsive actions take over your daily life. OCD is the problem behind the behavior. It's like being stuck in a horrible thought-process carousel you can't get off. It's the spaghetti junction of brain disorders. You KNOW you need to leave the road you're on, but you just can't find the exit.

My OCD was never about cleanliness. To be honest, I hate washing and find it a waste of time. I don't need to have a pristine house to feel happy. My OCD was much stranger than that. My OCD IS much stranger than that. It's still there, but I manage it.

I have intrusive-thought OCD. The best way to describe this is that a thought gallops into my brain. A horrible thought. A thought that makes me believe I could be the worst person alive. A person capable of carrying out the most appalling acts of violence.

When I was younger, I didn't just let that thought gallop out of my brain again. I got on top of it and I rode it obsessively. It was a mental illness rodeo.

I'd see someone in the street and have the most terrible intrusive thought about killing them or hitting them on the head. These thoughts would not give me any pleasure—they were like a horror film. Their detail was immense, and they would send me into a spiral of horror wondering what sort of monster I was. Sometimes these thoughts were so terrible, and so appalling, they were like a knife slicing into my brain. They'd make me yell out in pain, which I'd blame on a back spasm or a period cramp. Sometimes I'd think I'd said something horrible to someone (I hadn't), hit someone (I hadn't), punched a child or a policeman (I hadn't), stuck my finger up to my headmistress and she'd seen and I was going to be expelled (I hadn't, so she hadn't, so I wasn't).

That last one happened on a Friday, and I worried for an entire weekend before Monday came around and reality confirmed that it was all in my head.

Even though I never did the crime, I made myself do the time.

My brain played poker with itself constantly. Sometimes it would say, *Unless you pray/hit yourself/touch something a certain amount of times, something awful will happen. Your mom will die/World War III will start/you will fail all your exams/all your friends will fall out with you/the thing that you've done that you know you haven't really done will turn out to be something that you actually have done.*

I'm only telling you part of it, because it could go on forever. It was torture.

OCD is a frightening and exhausting condition. It feels like your brain is constantly shouting at you and blurting out new commands that you have to follow so that YOU CAN BE GOOD AND HAPPY AND SAFE. But in reality, OCD locks you in a cycle of unhappiness. In its grip, I felt like the most horrible, inappropriate person on the planet.

I didn't tell anybody about any of this. If you think you're the devil but you're also trying to take take your exams and succeed in school, you keep it under wraps. I had endless excuses. When I was having a really bad day, I used to say I had stomachache. Good old tummy ache. It can take doctors AGES to find out what is really wrong, and I had a real history of gastro problems. A hot water bottle was my constant companion. I'd say my gut was on fire, when really it was my head that was exploding.

The problem was, my methods of coping were not helping or curing my condition. Therefore, to some degree, I let OCD shape my life. I can give you a specific example. It always got really bad around exam time. I finished one of my French exams about fifteen minutes early.

Then a voice (it felt like GOD) popped into my head and said, "If you don't go and pray NOW, hit yourself, and then wash your hands twice, you'll fail this exam."

However, if you wanted to pee during an exam, a teacher would wait outside the toilet to check you weren't cheating. So this conversation started in my head:

You need to do all the rituals to pass the exam.

But the teacher will hear me praying and hitting myself and think I'm mad.

Doesn't matter. You need to do it.

I can't, though.

OK, fail. I am telling you what you need to do to pass and you won't listen.

But I've—

No. Go and do it. Or you know what will happen.

This continued until the end of the exam, when I rushed to the toilet and performed the ritual in private. I didn't check my exam paper and realized later I'd mixed up the French word for "shopwindow" with the word for "monkey," or something. But that's what OCD does. It stops you from being the best you can be, and from doing the sensible stuff.

I hope someone reading this who has previously thought they were a terrible person now realizes they are dealing with OCD. Here are some other symptoms that might point to you having obsessive compulsive disorder:

The clue is in the name—

An obsession with a compulsion to do something.

This can be:

Cleaning. It's not about having a tidy house. It's about feeling panic and mental pain when there is even a tiny piece of dirt in the place OR having a lengthy daily ritual of cleaning that is stopping you from doing other things.

Hand washing. This can come from a fear of germs and the feeling that you have to wash your hands to stay safe. Your hands may become sore, chapped, and red-raw from being washed so much, but you still have to keep doing it.

Having things in a certain order and getting very distressed when they are not in that order.

Feeling that if things are not done in a certain way, something terrible will happen.

Having the sort of intrusive thoughts I described. Thoughts that make you feel like you are the worst person on earth, and you have to do something to make it better.

Any thought process that you feel is controlling you, and forcing you into behaviors that upset you or that you know are unhealthy.

What I Did/Still Do to Make It Better

You'll notice the use of both the past and the present tense here. There's a reason for that. My OCD still tries to take control, and I still need to have a firm handle on it.

I'm convinced that had I tackled it sooner, this would not be the case. But I didn't. In fact, I had these severe thought processes from the age of eight up to about the age of twenty-eight. That's a long time of coping and covering up.

If you have these thoughts, and you're recognizing these behaviors in yourself, please, please talk to someone. This is the sort of condition that makes people feel ashamed to seek help. I felt a deep fear and embarrassment to even admit to some of the things that I'd been thinking, at first. Now I've just told everyone. Balls. I wasn't evil. I was ill.

Get Some Counseling

When I did eventually admit all to a fantastic counselor, she told me something very interesting. She said that there was evidence that continuing the behaviors of OCD over a long period of time can cause a chemical shift in your brain. This makes the mind believe that OCD is the normal way to be, and is why it's so hard to break out of. The GREAT news is that with practice and therapy this CAN be cured, controlled, and reversed. With a counselor, you can share all the stuff that's distressing you and work out a way together to make your mind better. This may involve all sorts of things, depending on the nature of your OCD. I know one person who had to touch the inside of a toilet bowl with her hands. No rubber gloves. Full on.

> **Dr. R. says:** *OCD can be treated with psychological therapy such as CBT, which helps you to understand your thoughts and feelings, plus exposure and response prevention (ERP), which helps you to face your thoughts (obsessions) without*

acting upon them (compulsive behavior). Medica-
tion can also help to treat OCD.

Each obsessive thought pattern will need different treatments, but here are some things you can try now:

Don't Mount the OCD Horse

Thoughts gallop into our brain all the time. You are not your thoughts. If I imagine kicking a puppy right now (horrible), it does not make me a horrible person. It makes me a person capable of imagining the pain and distress of an animal. That's a good thing. That's empathy. When a compulsive thought comes into your brain, try to let it bolt right through your mind. Let the thought be what it is—just a thought. It is not YOU. It is actually a chemical collection of electrons and neurons firing off. It is not your soul. It is a thought. Let thoughts go. Even the best brains sometimes fire off random crap. Even the kindest people sometimes have bad thoughts. This is what it is to be human. It would probably be simpler to be a penguin— but there's the cold to contend with, and the constant raw fish would get boring after a while . . .

I don't know why my brain just burped up penguins, but it did. See? The nature of our minds is that they are all a bit random. We are all linked by that.

Test Your Doom Theories

Your brain currently thinks your obsessive thoughts are keeping you safe in some way. They almost certainly

aren't, so a good, and very courageous, thing to do is to test them.

That means not doing what they tell you.

Terrifying. I know.

I can give you an example from today:

My husband has taken our little boy to work so I can write.

My brain said, *Unless you tap the table thirty-six times, they will die in a horrible road accident or your son will choke on the necklace that he's wearing.*

Those are pretty high stakes. Should I just do it and be safe?

No. For two very good reasons. It's just my OCD puking up some nonsense. It's an itch in my brain. If I do the ritual, I scratch the itch in my mind and, as with many conditions, scratching it makes the problem worse. My thoughts are just thoughts. My rituals do not make anyone safe. I have to acknowledge that there are things beyond my control.

When you accept that your thought processes are wrong, you can stop fighting yourself and end the spiral into doom and disaster.

Dismantling your entire thought process can be very frightening, and most of us will absolutely need professional support as we go through this. It's very hard to do on your own, and it takes practice. Day after day, hour by hour. But once you start seeing that terrible things don't happen when you don't do your rituals, your brain starts to understand that your OCD thinking is flawed and wrong. It can take a long time and a lot of bravery to conquer

OCD, but when you do manage to get on top of it, you'll feel so FREE and STRONG.

Update: My husband and son have just gotten home. My husband is moaning that I've drunk all the coffee (HELLO! I AM WRITING!) and my son wants me to play *Super Mario Kart*. All is well. See!

Distraction

Sometimes it's good to counter OCD thoughts by distracting your brain with other things. Get a passion. A bored brain is a dangerous brain. Make stuff. Craft stuff. Learn stuff. Song lyrics—I'm unbeatable. It's harder for an OCD brain burp to get through when you are feasting on the best of Beyoncé's words. Whatever. Give your mind a distraction. Give your brain something else to think about.

I see my OCD as something to keep on top of. I have to be very aware of my limitations. Now that I'm a bit older, I know just how much I can push myself. I don't always get it right. When I don't and I overload, I practice what I preach—I give myself a break. I also remember one very important thing—it's perfectly normal to imagine pushing someone you don't like off an incredibly high building. What isn't normal is doing it. The great news for OCD sufferers is that we are statistically less likely to be violent than other people AND there is no correlation between OCD and crime.

See. You're OK. You're not terrible. It can be sorted out. Just don't wait like I did. Two decades is a very long time to feel lousy about yourself. It was a waste. It stopped me from doing things. It sapped me of time and energy, and it was NEEDLESS. Get some help. You can tame your brain and do beautiful dressage with it. *(Dressage is a form of horse training and riding. I also like horses as well as planes. Sorry. They are cool, though. I love that eyes-on-the-side-of-the-face thing. And neighing. Nothing like a massive neigh.)*

"THEY WON'T SHUT UP"

Psychosis

Of all the conditions I talk about in this book, psychosis might be easily the most misunderstood.

So it's probably easier to start with what psychosis isn't. It's not about being a "psycho"—someone who hurts people, or someone who is two people in one body like the Incredible Hulk/David Banner or Dr. Jekyll and Mr. Hyde. Psychosis is far more complicated and sophisticated than that. The way in which the word is used has muddied how we see sufferers of the condition. It reminds me how careful we have to be with language. Not because we are "snowflakes" or overly sensitive, but because by using the wrong words, we foster ignorance and create unnecessary panic and incorrect opinions.

I should start by saying that I've never had serious or recurrent psychosis, but I did have a very definite instance of it in my teens, and I think that helps me to understand the condition a bit. It was all based around my nan putting milk in my tea.

That's weird. It's fine to laugh. It was shortly before I was hospitalized for a nervous breakdown. The fact that beverages partly sent me over the edge makes me smile in a dark-humor kind of a way. Cups of tea should not be threatening, but mental illness can turn even the simplest thing into something really dreadful.

At my most unwell, I lived in a state of constant paranoia. The easiest way to explain it is that everywhere I looked I saw evidence that I was being slowly killed. There was none, but thoughts in my brain weren't flowing together properly. My nan adored me, but my ailing mind created its own reality.

The problem in this case was that my nan watered down milk. This seems like a strange thing to do, but it was for a very good reason. She had lived through some very lean times in her life, including rationing in World War II, and watering down milk made it last longer. It did. It just also tasted funny. It tasted different. It tasted like she was trying to poison me. It tasted like death.

My nan was the sweetest woman in the world. This was a fact. She loved me. This was a fact. She would never have tried to hurt me. This was a fact.

None of these facts mattered. Reality did not matter. This different-tasting milk was proof that my head was right. But had my nan not watered down the milk, my brain would have found something else to confirm my beliefs. That's the nature of psychosis.

Luckily, I told my mom. Ironically I thought my nan trying to kill me was a sign that NAN was mentally ill. My mom told my doctors this, and they told me I was ill.

What Psychosis Might Feel Like

The difficulty of the symptoms of psychosis is, as I've shown, when you suffer from it, the unreal can seem very, very real. It can therefore be very difficult to realize that you are ill.

Here are some clues:

Your thoughts and beliefs seem to be at odds with what everyone else is telling you is fact.

Things aren't fitting together. They aren't flowing in the way they normally would. It's hard to think clearly. Everything in the world seems to be centered around you. This can feel like people are staring at you or talking about you—even strangers in the street.

You feel as though there are voices in your head giving you instructions or talking to you. They may be nice or unpleasant, but they feel or sound different from you.

You're seeing things that no one else can see. These need not be full-on hallucinations; sometimes you glimpse or sense something.

> **Dr. R. says:** *Psychosis is when someone interprets or perceives things in a different way from the reality. Symptoms of psychosis can include hallucinations (hearing or seeing things that are not there) or delusions (a strong belief that is out of touch with reality). Schizophrenia is a mental illness in which episodes of psychosis can occur.*

What Causes Psychosis?

It's not always simple to work out what is causing an episode of psychosis. It could be a number of things. Sometimes it's triggered by things like drug use, prolonged insomnia, or a reaction to a stressful event or series of events. It can be the symptom of an illness or, rarely, a sign that the brain is being disrupted by something like a tumor.

How to Cope with Psychosis

Psychosis is treated medically with antipsychotic medication, or psychological therapy such as CBT, or a combination of both. However, there are also some things you can do to help yourself.

If you are diagnosed with psychosis, it's important to have a solid network of family and friends around you.

If they too are mindful of your illness, they can help you keep as well as possible. Opting for a healthy lifestyle is also a good idea—a frankly obscenely healthy diet and lots of exercise can only help.

Likewise, and this is a choice I've had to make and will talk more about later, you're going to have to be super careful about all types of drugs. Legal and illegal. Even if you're feeling well, your brain is too finely tuned (like a magnificent orchestral harp) to have extra chemicals to cope with. Some people can get away with drinking alcohol or taking recreational drugs with no bad effects at all. You can't. Sorry. Life's not fair. That's the way it is.

I sound like a total nag, but I'm in the same boat. Honestly.

It's good to be aware if anyone in your family has had psychosis. Doctors now believe that these conditions can be passed down through families. If you feel that things aren't right and you're armed with that knowledge, you'll be on red alert for any symptoms. Early intervention means you can get help before your brain is too muddled.

I remember many, many years ago a ten-minute program on television presented by a man who had suffered with psychosis and schizophrenia. It was the sort of thing they showed on a Sunday where I lived, before the news. This was the mid-eighties I think, and no one admitted they suffered from mental illnesses then. There wasn't so much stigma as TOTAL DENIAL that things like that even existed. However, this guy came on in a trilby hat explaining he had suffered from schizophrenia and that he'd managed to get through it and create amazing art. He ended by singing a song about accentuating the positive. It was to this day one of the most inspirational things I've seen. He was amazing.

There's no reason you can't be amazing either. Psychosis can be a really difficult and isolating condition, but it can also be managed very successfully. And yes, you do get to educate the ignorant on what the term actually means. Feel free to lecture. You'll be doing the world a great service.

"BUT IT MAKES ME FEEL BETTER"

Self-harm

I really want to talk candidly about self-harm. It's something that people sometimes do when they have distressing feelings and thoughts and they don't know how to handle them, BUT it's self-destructive both mentally and physically.

LET ME JUST REITERATE THIS—
SELF-HARM IS HARMFUL.
PLEASE DON'T DO IT.

YOU DESERVE BETTER.
You REALLY do.

We need to find better ways to cope. If someone else did that to you, it would be assault. They'd be arrested.

We all know it's not the right thing to do, so why do any of us do it? Why did I do it?

In my case, at the time, I felt it made absolute sense to translate the agony in my brain into something real. This was nonsense, but I remember that's how it felt. The mess that was the traffic jam in my head needed a release. I HATED ME. It almost felt like my brain was demanding it. I did it, and it hurt. It really hurt, and afterward there was this strange feeling of . . .

Not relief. Not happiness. Not anything. I just didn't feel as bad as I had before. And sometimes I felt that I deserved it. (I didn't.)

I kept it secret for years. Scars can be covered up. Bruises can be blamed away. Burns—that's a harder one. Oh, this is a dreadful admission, but I put matches out on my arm. I mean W-T-actual-F? It's the burns that got me caught.

I had a lovely friend at my university. He was the best— he was kind, protective, funny, and sweet. At the time, I just really wanted a big brother, and that's what I got.

This lovely guy saw my arm full of little black marks. I

gave him some prime bull, but he saw straight through it. His reaction has stayed with me. He wasn't angry, he was quite matter of fact, and he asked me one very important question:

"Why do you do that to yourself?"

This was, and is, a very good question. How to explain? I was so full of emotion and in pain and I couldn't handle it. I felt overwhelmed.

It's a good question to ask yourself too. You might be self-harming because you are legitimately full of anger and rage at someone or something. In which case, harming yourself is completely counterproductive.

Or perhaps you don't like yourself? Give yourself a break, will you, and stop it. Self-harm does not help you to feel better about yourself. In fact, it has the opposite effect—you're basically telling your head you deserve to be physically hurt.

If it's about relieving tension and feelings you don't quite understand, there are far, far, far better ways.

Trust me. Self-harm creates more problems than it ever solves. I thought self-harm was helping me to survive, and get through all the pain and rage I had inside me. But it was a short-term fix, and short-term fixes don't fix long-term problems. And in my case, it has created another long-term issue.

Scars.

Now that I live somewhere that is sometimes very hot, covering up isn't always an option.

My self-harm scars make me feel incredibly self-conscious. It's not the issue of having an imperfection on my skin. I feel no shame at all about my gall bladder scar. It's the needless scars I'm embarrassed about because I might as well have written a massive sign on my arm saying, "I hate myself and I think I'm worth nothing." It's a permanent reminder of how little I thought of myself, and I don't feel that way anymore.

The marks sometimes draw glances. You know when you just catch people looking? I can't get a tan. It makes them look even worse. I look like a self-harming leopard. How could I have done that to myself? If only I had given myself a break. I was doing OK. I was doing the best that I could.

What I'm trying to say to you again is

PLEASE STOP SELF-HARMING.
DO SOMETHING ELSE INSTEAD.

Here are some suggestions:

Talk to Someone

Why are you self-harming? What emotion is making you do that to yourself? What can you do to change that? How can you feel better about yourself? Why are you being so hard on yourself? Sometimes talking things through with someone you trust can make the answers to these questions clearer, and help you to work through things.

Likewise, if you're self-harming as a way to cope with pressure from school or work, tell someone. You may feel that you cannot cope with all the demands being put on you, but there are ways to organize your life to make things easier (see the chapter about anxiety and stress).

It's very difficult to carry the burden of a problem on your own. Vocalizing that problem, just hearing yourself say the words, can release so much pressure from you. The person you are talking to may have a suggestion as to how you can cope with the issue. Sometimes just the act of them listening can really help.

If your self-harming is a response to abuse, you need specialist care. Find someone you trust and tell them what happened. It doesn't matter when it happened either; it could have been years ago—you deserve to be looked after.

Do Something Else with Your Emotions

When that self-harm impulse comes on, act on it positively. Go for a massive walk that makes your legs ache. Go for a run. If you find leaving the house difficult, put on some music and dance. I still do this for exercise. I probably look like a deranged octopus, but who cares? It expends all that energy. Walk. Dance. Pound the streets. All this will work your body and make you ache but in a great way that doesn't harm or scar you.

Write Down How You Feel

I know I would say this, but write it down. Write down all the feelings. Not online. Somewhere that's just yours. Somewhere safe. Write down how you feel. Write down what you want to do, BUT DON'T DO IT. This will help in two ways. It will relieve some of the tension inside you AND it could even help the people who are trying to help you. If you can't say how you feel but can show them what you've written, they might be able to help in a way that's more useful to you.

An "I Feel Like Self-Harming" Safe-Word Friend

Self-harm is not a new thing. Lots of us did it. We just felt we couldn't talk about it. I did it. I'm probably old enough to have you as a child. And if I was your mom, I'd want to know you felt the way I did and I'd want to help you too. Seriously. I'd want to be there for you to tell you YOU CAN make things better and that this WILL end. You don't have to self-harm.

If you feel you can't tell a parent (and I realize some people may genuinely have crap parents), tell another adult or someone older you trust. They may have felt exactly like you at some point themselves, and understand far more than you realize.

Tell them what you're doing. They might be upset, but they shouldn't be angry. Have a code word between you that means you feel like self-harming. When you use this code word (it could be something as simple as "melon"), they know you need distraction and love. They'll know you need help. When they hear it, you can talk through how you feel and what you feel like doing to yourself in complete confidence. It could help you get through that moment when you feel like harming yourself.

Suicide and Suicidal Thoughts

Suicide and suicidal thoughts are a medical emergency. If you're feeling like you want to take your own life, you NEED to speak to someone URGENTLY.

I need to tackle that first. Put this book down, and get on the phone with an organization like the Samaritans right now. (In the US you can call 1-800-273-TALK or 1-800-273-8255.) Then, when you're feeling like you can, read this section and hopefully you'll understand why.

It could be that you feel trapped in a situation that you can't see any other way out of. Perhaps you've been stuck there for a long time, and nothing is working to make you feel better.

It could be that your brain is misfiring a load of chemicals that are making you feel that way. Whatever the cause, you need help. PLEASE get it. Whoever you are—you DO have options.

I read something the other day railing against the phrase sometimes said to suicidal people—"Don't do anything stupid."

I can understand why people get angry at this. Someone who is suicidal isn't going to be helped by such a simple, glib phrase. Dismissing suicide as "stupid" doesn't help either. But the thing is, the people who love you and care for you know that you have options. If you're feeling hopeless, I can promise you that unless you are currently in the middle of a zombie apocalypse (and to be fair, watching *The Walking Dead* proves you can even survive THAT!) there is nothing that you can't get through.

You have no idea how strong you are.

You DO have options.

I've had periods where I've felt incredibly low, but if I'd taken my own life, it would have been stupid. The pain did end. The illness was tackled. I managed to cope with who I was and am.

I live in another country, I've had several very lovely careers, I've had a beautiful son, I've nearly been shot in the Czech Republic while singing the theme tune to *Heidi*, I've done unspeakable (and very enjoyable) things on a

Scottish golf course, and I think I've managed to bring some happiness to other people's lives.

I'm not a naturally strong person, but you can learn to be strong. I've listened to advice and I've learned to cope.

I know, at my worst times, I would never have believed all this. When I was in such terrible despair, what I have now would have seemed ridiculous and impossible.

Forgive the obvious, but if I were dead, that would have been it. Suicide is the end of hope.

But it's more than that.

Suicide has a terrible legacy—it doesn't just end your life; it's like throwing a stone in the river of so many people's lives. That ripple goes on and on. You leave the people who love you with so many regrets and so much sadness. This isn't a guilt trip; it's a fact. I want to tell you about my friend who committed suicide. Let's call her Kitty.

Kitty was wonderful. She was beautiful inside and out. Clever, kind, acerbic, supportive, and very, very funny. She was the best person to be at a party with. She once caught me when I slid off the back of the sofa with a wineglass in my hand. We went to the US together and shared a room. One night I actually bored myself to sleep by talking about the best pizza I'd ever eaten. I woke up to her laughing her head off about it. Which set me off on a giggling fit because I'd cured both jet lag and insomnia with my own tediousness.

I have so many brilliant memories of her, but they are also very painful now because she took her own life. I try to just remember my wonderful sparky friend, but the tragedy of her final moments creeps into my head.

I think, *What could I have done? What could I have said?* The answer is almost certainly nothing. No one was responsible for Kitty's suicide. It was her decision. That doesn't stop you wondering, though, or thinking about the waste of such an amazing contributor to this world.

So I'm asking you, if you do feel suicidal, PLEASE talk to somebody. Don't let your memory be one that makes people feel so sad. You are worth so much more than that.

And if you have lost somebody to suicide, you need help too. Suicide brings up a whole range of feelings. Honestly I felt furious at Kitty for a long time. I yelled at her. I lost it with her even though she wasn't there. Sometimes grief does odd things to you. Never be afraid to seek help for coping with those feelings. They can be very complicated and difficult to handle. I realized this when I found myself shouting at a packet of crackers in a kitchen cupboard. Specialized grief counseling is available if something like this happens to you—talking things through can help you come to terms with everything.

"I DON'T FEEL ANYTHING"

Depression

Depression isn't just feeling sad. Sometimes depression is not feeling anything at all.

I'm not going to use myself as an example in this chapter, because I don't think I *am* a very good example. My depression was a result of my OCD and anxiety issues. It's logical that I felt sad, desperate, and depressed when I felt so dreadful about myself, but depression wasn't my main illness. So, I'm going to use my mom instead.

My mom has bipolar disorder. She hates that term, though, and calls it manic depression. If you have depression, you get to call it what you like. British prime minister and wartime leader Winston Churchill called his depression "the Black Dog."

(It's worth pointing out here that someone with severe depression managed to defend the free world at a time when many people regarded Hitler as "sane.")

My mom has had depression for many years. Decades. And, because of that, she's learned to express herself and live with it very well.

She can't remember when it started. She describes to me feeling like she's had odd moods since she was very young. Depression in anyone can be the result of genetics, or a chemical imbalance in the brain, or it can be a very logical response to horrible things that have happened, or are happening, in your life. Some people become depressed after using drugs, after an illness, or completely out of the blue.

Because my mom is now in her seventies, how she has been treated demonstrates the different ways people with mental illness have been treated through the years. And it's really interesting. Not so long ago, people with depression just "kept quiet." There was an enormous stigma attached to talking about anything that could be remotely perceived as "weak." If you did, you were told to pull yourself together. This is what I term "useless curtain treatment." Telling a depressive to pull themself together (like a pair of curtains) is like telling someone who has broken their leg to just will their fracture to mend. It just doesn't work. They need to see a doctor.

Eventually my mom was prescribed therapy. She was

lucky. I think our family doctor—despite always wearing a tweed three-piece suit and a pocket watch—was really a forward thinker on the issue. He was an ex–military doctor. Yet again I have to say that people who have seen some truly dreadful things can actually be the most understanding when it comes to mental illness. They "get" how badly a head can hurt and how deeply it can be affected by traumatic events. With a combination of that therapy and her own experience, my mom has learned to manage her condition.

I can tell when my mom is about to have an episode of depression. The best way to describe it is to imagine a shop closing up at night. It's all in her eyes. It's like the security blinds are coming down. There is blankness. There's no wailing or crying. There's a silence. Not a calm, comfortable silence, an eerie one. And then she disappears. She can function still. She can do the basics, but my mom is gone. Does that make sense? There's just this shell.

And then she comes back. It's usually after a few days. Sometimes she's her normal self, and sometimes she comes back in a manic way. In the past, her manias have led her to do some silly things. Marrying a Moroccan bodybuilder who couldn't speak English and having a picture of him flexing his muscles tattooed on her bottom, we can now clearly see, was probably the result of a manic episode. But manic people are fun. My normally very quick-witted mom on a mania is like a cross between Stephen Fry and a lioness. She's ferociously quick. You could put her on any comedy panel show and she'd demolish everyone. She's

INCREDIBLE. And then the depression comes back and her shop shuts again for a time.

I asked my mom last night what her depression feels like, and she described it in a very interesting way.

She said it's like a muffling of all your senses. It feels like your body and soul are full of cotton wool. It's frightening too. She said that sometimes she can walk from one end of the room to the other and it just comes on. She can feel it approaching, but she can't do anything about it. It's like a wrecking ball. She can see it swinging toward her, but it's impossible to stop. She has always still managed to go to work and paint a face on. She has always still managed to be a great mom to me. BUT inside she often felt utterly numb or in despair.

This is just my mom's experience. Everyone's depression feels different. But I've included it because depression sufferers are usually portrayed as people lying in bed looking sad, which can be true, but depression comes in all shapes and sizes.

Depression can also feel like this:

Not Being Able to Cope
A need to withdraw from the world and do nothing.

Not Wanting to Participate
A lack of interest in everything and everyone around you.

A Constant Sadness
It's a sadness that has nothing to do with what's happening in the world or any event that's happening in

your life. Sadness is often an entirely appropriate reaction to the world. There's nothing wrong with feeling sad, and it doesn't need to be medicated or "fixed." But the sadness that comes with depression is like a permanent "heavy" feeling in every part of your brain and body. Like my mom says, someone could give you a check for a million dollars and tell you every problem in your life was fixed and you'd STILL feel sad.

Irrational Anger and Irritability
You have no patience with anyone. Even people you love and like.

Feelings of Despair
Like the weight of the world is on top of you.

Fear of Anything and Everything
But you're not sure why. There's nothing to be frightened of.

An Absence of Feeling
A numbness. It feels like you're dead inside and nothing has a point. When my mom saw the Dementors in the Harry Potter series, I told her they were based on J. K. Rowling's experiences of depression and she said, "YES! THAT. IS. IT!" Depression can feel as though your soul is being sucked out. It takes "you" away.

Pointlessness
Nothing seems to matter. Perhaps things that meant a lot to you before your depression mean nothing anymore. You don't see the point in doing anything.

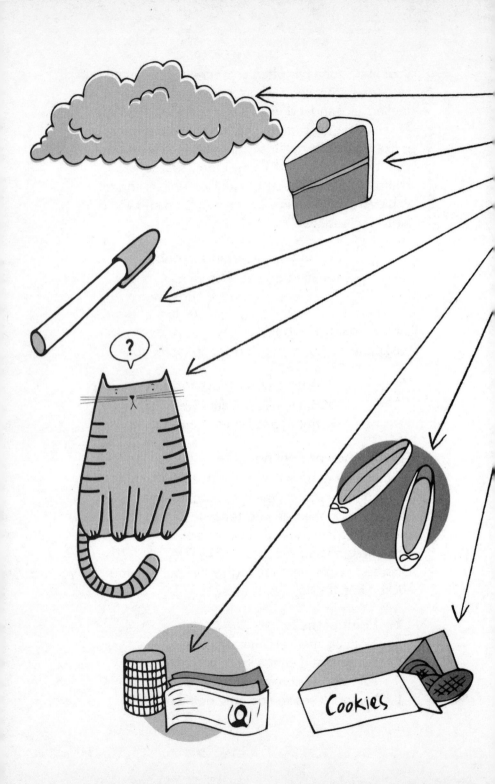

WHAT YOU CAN DO ABOUT DEPRESSION

Counseling

Talking to someone won't fix a chemical imbalance, just as talking to someone doesn't fix a broken leg, BUT . . .

It could give you a time and a place to be honest and share your feelings. Sometimes we don't want to do that with the people we love because we are scared of upsetting or worrying them. Counselors, psychologists, and psychiatrists are trained professionals who listen but don't judge. They can help you manage your illness and the reactions of the people around you. They can be on your side. It's important with a disease that can make you feel so lonely to also feel like you have people in your squad.

Take It by the Moment

My mom focuses on getting through her depression moment by moment. She tries to get her bearings by concentrating on something. Anything. A crossword. The hedgehogs in her garden. Sometimes she will lie on her bed and just look at the radiator in her bedroom. For the next five minutes, she'll focus on the curves of it, how it looks, and the warmth it's giving off. She diverts her head. I'm not suggesting you start staring at all the heating appliances in your home, but lying down, focusing, and letting your head concentrate on something else (perhaps something very dull) can help you get through the very worst of the depression.

Remind Yourself That You Will Get Better

This. Keep repeating it. A great phrase is "This too shall pass" and it shall.

I could quote all the memes in the world here, but I do also love Winston Churchill's "If you're going through hell, keep going." As someone who suffered with depression and who was in a world war, he understood what "hell" meant and how you could get through it.

#TeamYou

Keep people around you who are sympathetic. Explain that you don't expect them to cure you or make you feel better. In fact, that can be absolutely the wrong thing to do. When my mom was ill, before I knew any better, I used to try to "cheer her up." (I know, I know. Stupid.) This included constant forced enthusiasm from me, jokes, really bad impressions that I thought were great, and generally following her around like an overexcited poodle. That's absolutely NOT what she needed. What she could actually have done with was me respecting the mental place that she was in. This could have been as simple as giving her space or practical help.

Don't be embarrassed to ask the people around you for help with the everyday stuff, like schoolwork. I remember when I was really ill, I missed a lot of school. A friend of mine lent me his politics study notes and told me to keep it as long as I liked. Actually, twenty-seven years later, I've still got it! At the time it really helped me catch up AND it helped me to feel like I was doing "normal" school things. It made me feel like I was part of things again and that was really important. You need people who can give you space and just let you "be." People who don't try to fix you but understand that you may need some company every so often. Perhaps just to binge a show together in silence. It doesn't matter. Find people who know you are not in a good place and can cope with that. Don't be afraid to talk to people about how you feel. Sometimes we really underestimate those around us, and sometimes the most unusual people can turn out to be very good and able in the trickiest situations. Trusting and opening up to people can be very difficult. But your friends and family will want to be there for you, and to help you, so give them the chance. And if you find it hard to express how you feel, why not give them this section of the book to read, as a conversation starter?

Simple Pleasures

These are things that give your mind a little piece of relief. It could be nature—a walk in the countryside can make you feel better even if you're a confirmed city dweller. It could be your favorite TV show. It could be music. Sometimes a song can be a way of explaining how you feel, HEAL parts of you, and talk for you without you having to open your mouth.

I remember after my time on a psychiatric ward I came out feeling like a complete and utter failure. I was defeated. Broken. I was in a rut and I couldn't see a way out. I was sitting in my bedroom looking out at a dirty gray street and feeling trapped. I was half listening to the radio and a song came on. It had a very distinctive opening—it sounded a bit Disney-ish and felt old and classic, like it should be on really thick, creamy old vinyl. Actually, at the time it was a new song and it wasn't the sort of thing I normally liked. But it caught my attention and I listened to it.

By the end, I was sobbing, because I felt it explained so much of what I was feeling and wanted to say but couldn't. It was a song by four Germans (with odd haircuts), but for me it was a release. I felt someone had seen inside my head and tried to make sense of it. That's what music can do. It demands so little of us, but we can get so much from it.

To this day when I don't feel too great, I put that song on and I feel better. I can't listen to it publicly, though, because I end up crying. And when people ask me if I'm OK, it's difficult to say, "Yes. I just listened to 'Keeping the Dream Alive' by Freiheit and it has touched a nerve." That's my song, though, and I love it. Find a tune you can rely on. My mom's is "Break My Stride" by Matthew Wilder. If you listen to that now, you'll just find a jolly bit of eighties pop cheese. It's not just that to my mom, though, and that's the point. It doesn't matter what it means to anyone else—it's what it means to you.

(By the way, I just listened to Freiheit at my desk and ended up crying again. It never fails. It's beautiful. It saved my life. Find your tune. Mom has just come in, looked at my face, and given me two Brazil nuts without a word. That's a lovely moment I wanted to share. Looking after each other sometimes doesn't need words.)

Exercise

I know I keep going on about exercise, but when I did my (very limited) training for the London Marathon, a completely lovely guy from the Territorial Army offered to help me. He was just about to go and do a tour of Iraq. He asked me to meet him at the local psychiatric hospital in the city where I lived.

When I got there, I asked him what he was doing. He explained that he was a volunteer and he helped the patients keep fit because it was such an important part of mental health. We then jogged around Leicester together. He explained that everyone's mental health can be helped by physical activity. This is because exercise releases hormones called endorphins. Endorphins are completely free, completely natural, and make you feel happier. As previously discussed, ANY exercise is good. Running, walking, dancing, yoga, jumping, Zumba—it doesn't matter what you do! Close the bathroom door, put a lock on, and rave on your toilet. It doesn't matter. Even if it starts with a gentle rock from side to side, just get moving. If all you can manage is to walk to the end of the street and back, that's totally fine. Build up. Anything is better than nothing.

Managing your exercise is like managing every aspect of your mental health—take it step by step.

Opposite Action

Opposite action is when you do exactly the opposite of what your brain is telling you to do. It's about acknowledging your feelings but not acting on them in the way your brain may be telling you to act. For example, you may feel furious and your first reaction maybe to shout and have a HUGE tantrum or meltdown. However, if you take the opposite action, you'll go and do something incredibly calming and relaxing instead. It's about not always doing what your brain is ordering you to do.

I've realized my mom has been inadvertently doing "opposite action" for years. With her depression, her brain regularly screamed at her to stay in bed and pull the duvet over her head. She didn't, though. She went to work. She became a union representative. She socialized. She did the opposite of what her head was telling her to do. It helped.

This technique can take a great deal of practice. It's like a muscle—it gets stronger the more you do it. It's definitely worth a try, though. It's a way to turn negative feelings into positive actions.

Volunteer

When you're on the mend, a great way to feel better about yourself is to GIVE BACK. I've said it before and I'll say it again. Volunteer. Find a place in your community where you can be useful. The beautiful thing about this is, you can help others while helping yourself. Sharing our experiences and knowledge with others builds the self-esteem and happiness of everyone involved. It's a fantastic thing to do when you feel well enough.

Medication

If you've been experiencing any of these feelings, please go and see your doctor. If you're not comfortable talking about your feelings, write them down, or take someone who can help you to vocalize what you're going through. Doctors don't care *how* they receive the information about your health, THEY JUST WANT TO HEAR IT.

Depression is a disease that we are still learning about. Every brain is different. Younger brains present different challenges too. They are still growing and changing. The doctor may prescribe a course of medication for you. However, certain medications that are appropriate for adults may not be appropriate for you. Your doctor will talk this through with you.

If you are prescribed antidepressants, they also take time to work—usually a couple of weeks or so. They can make you feel quite wobbly and disorientated at the start, but this feeling soon goes. When I've taken antidepressants in the past, I've felt like emotionally I've been walking up and down hills and somehow I've been put on more even ground. It's easier to do things. I feel more "level." This is what medication does. It fixes the chemical imbalance and smooths things in your brain.

If You're Feeling Really Desperate, Call the Twenty-Four-Hour People

Depression can make you feel like you have no options to live happily. It can make you feel suicidal. I just want to tell you about a desperate, terrible time I had, and how the Samaritans helped me through it.

Different countries in the world have different suicide prevention organizations. In the US, there's the Suicide Prevention Lifeline you can chat online at suicidepreven tionlifeline.org or 1-800-273-8255. I already mentioned the Samaritans. They are fantastic and have centers in thirty-eight countries. They are there to listen, and sometimes you just need to be heard by someone. You know you can't be fixed in one phone call, and you're not expecting to be. You just want another human to be there and to talk to.

The night I rang them I was in my second year of university, and I was really unwell. I felt that if I failed my exams, I'd have to leave university, the world would end, and then I'd truly be up the cul-de-sac of total failure and disaster.

I was also in a very unhealthy relationship, which didn't help. All I'd wanted was a boyfriend, but the one I had just wasn't very nice to me. I wasn't overweight anymore, but being thin hadn't solved anything. I still felt dreadful about myself. I kept thinking about being in a psychiatric ward, which made me feel like a freak and a failure. When I was a young teen, I was molested, and the memory of this was haunting me. I kept thinking about how dreadful it had made me feel. How dreadful I felt. I was panicking about the fact that in less than twelve hours I had to write about medieval English texts, and how little I knew about the eleventh-century book *The Peterborough Chronicle*. (It was something about monks getting hammered in a Cambridgeshire. Typical Saturday-night stuff, just really old.)

In short, my head was a food blender of problems. I couldn't stop it from swirling around and pulping my thoughts up. And I couldn't see a way out of it all. But I knew in that moment I needed someone to talk to. So I called the Samaritans and I got through to Hazel.

I'm going to use her real name. She deserves the acknowledgment. Hazel listened as I sobbed and sobbed. I don't think I made sense for forty-five minutes. I just cried until my face ached. All Hazel heard was tears and snot and nose blows, but she was listening.

Eventually I went through everything. I think the phone call lasted for more than two hours. Hazel listened, comforted me, and just acknowledged all my pain.

Because she was so worried about me, she then asked if she could call me back to check that I was OK.

She did later on. And I was. I got through. The crisis passed. The clouds cleared. I managed to pass the exam. The other things took longer to fix, but I realized something vital.

I wasn't alone.

At the end of the phone, there was someone there twenty-four hours a day. There's a list of contacts for the Samaritans, and other organizations like them, at the end of this book. Day or night, you never have to suffer alone.

There are people who give their time to make people like me, in such a state of distress and despair, feel better. The very fact that somebody could be so kind gave me hope.

Depression can be very cruel. It can make you feel and think a whole host of terrible things. But please don't forget there are people who can help. Depression is a bastard you don't have to deal with alone.

My mom has just said to me, "You haven't made me out to be pitiful, have you?" I've assured her that this isn't the case. Anyone who lives with depression is not pitiful; they are amazing and they should be treasured. If that's you—you have my total respect. Be kind to yourself and look after yourself.

"I'VE GOT A ZIT THE SIZE OF MADRID!"

How to Wear and Cope with Your Diagnosis

When it comes to mental health, I think we are living in slightly better times than we were a few decades ago—in terms of both caring for people suffering from mental illness and reducing the stigma around it.

Don't yell at me. Let me explain.

I know it sounds like a big claim. And don't get me

wrong—some mental health care, especially for young people, is still really lacking. Often it's just BAD. I'm very aware that some people still have to travel too far to get the appropriate treatment. I know some people have to FIGHT to get the right treatment, or any treatment at all. That's not right. We all know it's not right.

But there are many great organizations that know this, and they are fighting for that to be recognized. THINGS ARE CHANGING. I PROMISE. You may not believe it, but there is now more understanding and help available. *(See the end of this book for a list of people who can help you. There is probably more care out there than you think, and much of it is very specialized.)*

There is still stigma, but not so long ago, there was something even worse—total silence.

When I was younger (and I'm not THAT old), no one told you about mental health or how to look after your brain. Only hearts and spleens and elbows went wrong. "Ladies" also had "Lady Problems"—you HAD to say this very quietly, as periods were a deeply embarrassing thing. No matter that they were partly responsible for the HUMAN RACE CONTINUING—bleeding was dirty and sanitary napkins were the size of sofa cushions.

People with mental health problems did exist, of course, but they were hidden away in institutions. These were often huge converted Victorian mansions, and some people spent most of their lives in them. Sometimes they didn't need to. They just got stuck in them and in a system that really didn't understand mental health issues. Mental illness was shameful—something to be hidden away. It certainly wasn't anything that you associated with success.

We know now, through their bravery in speaking up, that some INCREDIBLE doctors, entertainers, builders, artists, comedians, businesspeople, traffic wardens, landscape gardeners, and charity shop volunteers who get their daughters amazing bargains (hello and thanks, Mom) have all suffered at one time or another with mental illness.

Mental illness does not have to stop YOU from doing what you want. Getting a diagnosis is not the end of your story. Often it's a great relief, it means you are finally going to get the care you need and deserve, but it still leaves you as YOU. You're in there. The illness may be a short- or long-term thing, but it isn't ALL of you.

You may feel you have a label. You may feel that other people have given you that label and you don't want it. It's a real shame, but, even now, after all these years and all the things that I've done, to some people I'm still (adopts small-town-gossip whisper tone) "that girl who went a bit funny. You know (puts hand up to head and swirls it round), nutty. Mad. Poor thing. Bit of an attention seeker, perhaps?"

I did hear that. Whatever. People can say what they like. In the end, what other people say or do is just noise. Blocking out criticism from those who don't really know you is an increasingly important skill. Your condition is only YOUR business, the business of the people who know and love you, and the business of the professionals who are helping you. The opinions of random people are completely irrelevant. Bat them away.

I've had to deal with some stuff for a very long time. I'd like to use an example from the dark old days that is actually a really great piece of advice.

When I was very young and all my odd behaviors started to appear, my mom took me to the doctor. She rattled off a list of some of the things I did. Poor old doctor. He was probably expecting something simple like tonsillitis. Instead he got this. My mom's full list of "Rae's worrying things":

> Wiggling my fingers constantly (still do this).

> Walking into walls in a trance. Not hitting the wall. Just going up and staring at it. It's when I'm having a total out-of-body intense daydream moment. (I still do this. My partner says, "Nice trip?" He's used to it now.)

> Holding my finger in front of my face, wiggling it and staring at it. (I rarely do this now.)

> Getting worked up about really odd things (see phobia chapter).

Hiding behind the sideboard when it rains (completely grown out of this).

When I do something I'm proud of, rocking back and forth over the thing that I've made and making a humming noise (don't think I do this now).

Hating any change to a set routine (better at this).

Not really sleeping (STILL an issue).

Not really relating to those around me. I spent my fifth birthday party in the toilet of the scout hut where it was being held. Bored. Really bored. And scared. (Much better with this.)

Obsessed with things. Has to listen to ALL the charts on the radio while holding salad tongs. If you disturb me, I have an uncontrollable tantrum. (I think this is a justifiable response to music being disturbed, but yeah, fair enough.)

I probably was/am on the Asperger's/autism/ADHD spectrum. I may have been a lot of things, but these "things" weren't widely discussed or spoken about, or perhaps even known about, then. So the doctor, who had very limited resources at his disposal, went quiet for a while.

Before I tell you what he said, let me remind you this was small-town Lincolnshire last century. As I've said before, childhood mental health problems didn't really exist. The doctor stared at me in a kindly way over his frankly huge and gorgeous desk full of compartments for metal prods and elastic bands (what did he use those for?) and said something that sounds quite harsh, but is actually quite true.

"She's probably just a bit different from lots of other children. You and her, Mrs. Earl, are going to have to find ways to manage it."

Manage it. It sounds really hard and clinical, doesn't it? But it was true at the time and it's still true now. Managing something just means getting the help that is available, accepting it, and THEN looking after yourself ALL THE TIME. You have to find a way to get on top of your brain and to manage it in a healthy way.

In that way, managing a mental illness is a bit like managing a zit.

That zit is always there. Sometimes it's under the skin and only you can feel it. It seems manageable. At other times, it erupts, it feels out of control, and you have to take special measures to cope with it.

People may want to talk about your zit. That's up to you. You may want to say, "This is my zit—deal with it." If you're not ready to talk about it with friends, family, and random people on buses, that is absolutely no problem either. It's worth pointing out here that talking about your zit will cause other people to react to it. You have no control over these reactions. It is fine to keep your zit private if you're getting adequate care. Just say "I'm not ready to talk about it yet."

You are not your zit. You are not your mental illness either. You are more than your condition. I can't say that enough. Don't feel your zit will stop you doing anything in the future. It's not the only thing about you. It's not the main thing about you. Don't let it define you.

Your zit is not a get-out-of-jail-free card. You have to be honest and ask yourself if you really can do what's being asked of you. Your zit cannot become a go-to excuse for anything you don't want to do. I used to do this, so I'm just being honest with you. Life felt like such a battle a lot of the time, I felt I deserved total freedom to call all the shots. This was wrong. Other people had zits too. Sometimes I used to say I felt unwell in my head when I was just slightly anxious at parties. This meant I made entire groups of people come home from things, which wasn't fair. My zit was not more important than everyone else's zit. Zits are everywhere, as is mental illness.

I repeat: Your job is to look after your head.

Keeping Your Head Healthy
as You Get Better

Your brain needs constant maintenance. You're like a car. You need tweaking, polishing, tune-ups, and regular refueling. And a shower every so often.

Transportation again. Sorry. Obsession.

Anyway, even if you're currently being refurbished by professionals, you still need to do your part. That includes telling them if their treatment isn't working for you AND looking after yourself generally. This is particularly important after a period of intensive treatment when you are becoming more independent. You need strategies in place so you can keep getting better and keep yourself in the best shape possible.

Coping with Triggering and
Being a Trigger Master

The basic problem with triggering is that the world is triggering. Triggers are anything that make you feel stressed, anxious, depressed, or unwell, or things that can trigger unhealthy thoughts and behaviors. For example, talking about calories and dieting can be very triggering to someone with an eating disorder.

The problem is, different things trigger different people. We can't get rid of butterflies and moths just because some people are frightened of them. We can't control the world around us, so we have to find ways and means of coping with it.

It all comes back down to you getting ahold of your head and making the right choices FOR YOU. This is both about the choices that we make when we are feeling mentally well and those absolutely VITAL choices we make when we are feeling unwell.

I've made some dreadful choices about triggering, and occasionally I still do. Let me give you a really recent example of something incredibly stupid I did when I wasn't feeling at my strongest. I REALLY should have known better. (I'll come to that later.)

The thing is, I've never been good with "dark downer endings" to movies or TV shows when I'm feeling anxious. When I'm mentally at full capacity, I LOVE them. I LOVE (SPOILER ALERT) the end of *Invasion of the Body Snatchers* when Donald Sutherland turns out to be a plant-based alien! I ADORE the way *Game of Thrones* just kills people off without warning you. I (and PLEASE BE CAREFUL WITH THIS FILM) think the Dutch film *Spoorloos* has one of the most horrifying YET UTTERLY BRILLIANT endings in the history of cinema.

That's on a good day.

But on a bad day watching any of those things is a BAD idea. Dark downer endings can trigger HUGE anxiety for me.

A few months ago, even though I was feeling a bit mentally "meh," I opted to watch Charlie Brooker's utterly magnificent series *Black Mirror*.

I'd been warned. I'd read ample pieces about how great it was and how mind-meltingly disturbing each episode could be, but I couldn't be stopped. I had huge cultural fear of missing out *(pathetic)*. I like telling people about amazing TV, films, and music *(that's your EGO, Rae—get over yourself!)* and I needed to see it. *(You didn't. People don't rely on you for their viewing recommendations and it wasn't going anywhere. Watch* Gilmore Girls *instead.)*

(The bits in parenthesis are the sane parts of me talking—but my brain wasn't listening to those.)

I watched the one everyone said was actually lovely, and it was. Then I watched another one, which was superb but a bit . . . worrying, and then I watched another. And then I had to lie down for an hour. Full-on anxiety attack triggered like an exploding bullet of head mess from a gun.

Chest tight. Breathless. Brain gone from meh to meltdown. ARGH! I'd failed to listen to my brain, even though it KNEW it would be triggered by such a show.

But my mind is just one mind in a million.

Should Charlie Brooker stop making *Black Mirror*? No.

Should *Black Mirror* be banned? No.

Should I be careful when I watch *Black Mirror* in the future? YES.

As much as you can, you need to learn to recognize the things that trigger you and avoid them. If something you can't avoid triggers you, you might benefit from counseling to identify why it's causing you so much distress. That way, you can develop coping mechanisms so that when you are presented with whatever triggers bad feelings, you can handle it without having a full meltdown.

A good thing to do is to make a note of what triggers

you and how it feels. The brain is always on the lookout to make connections. That's how it uses the senses to make sense of itself. If I smell hot dogs, I feel ill (long and unpleasant story involving a badly timed snack and a fair ride), but if I smell lavender, I'm triggered into thinking of my nan and her frankly world-class roast dinners. If you can understand why you're being triggered, you can comfort your brain. The badly triggered brain is like a puppy that's just heard a vacuum cleaner for the first time. It needs some reassurance. It's up to you to give it, and to put a plan in place for the next time it happens.

Give It Some Diva

No, the world doesn't revolve around you, but it doesn't hurt to do a full Mariah Carey every so often. Divas know what they want, what they don't want, and what makes them happy. And they're not afraid to go after it. Sometimes you have to be a diva to keep your head healthy.

I'm not suggesting demanding tiny dogs in your dressing room (although that would be nice) or getting someone to take out all the orange M&M's before you will even consider eating a bowlful. I'm suggesting you make sure you tell people when you've REALLY reached your limits and you need time out. Every day for at LEAST TEN MINUTES, I put my phone down and I lie on my bed in total silence thinking about winning the equestrian three-day event at the Olympics. My horse is magnificent, the crowd goes wild, and Clare Balding is in tears at my brilliance. She hugs me and tells me it's the best show jumping she's ever seen. Please note—I've only really ever been on a donkey on the beach at a small coastal town. It doesn't matter! This is my disconnect diva moment. I go fully into MY world.

By the way, if some of the nature of my advice seems a little bit contradictory to what helps you, that's because everyone's brain responds to different things. What works for you may be the opposite of what works for someone else. I just think everything is worth a try.

Brainbin

This is a simple way to deal with horrible thoughts, or with anything that is distressing you. Get yourself a trash can. A small office-sized one will do. Or a giant industrial one if you're feeling REALLY fed up.

Get some paper and splat down all the things that are bothering you.

SCREW and RIP UP THESE BITS OF PAPER and, with REAL FORCE, throw them in the bin. Maybe do it from the other side of the room, BUT WATCH THEM FLY IN. Throw all that horrible head stuff IN THE GARBAGE. I don't think it's going to magic these worries away, but it's so satisfying to see all that NONSENSE in a bin.

You can then take all these thoughts and put them out with recycling, thereby also being environmentally friendly.

You may also like to use a paper shredder. Someone I know uses their bad thoughts as bedding for their pet rat. That's good too. This whole ritual is a particularly

satisfying thing to do at night. It's like throwing away all your bad thoughts before you go to bed.

Diaries

I know. This isn't a surprise, is it? Sorry to be predictable. It's just I really believe they work, and will never be replaced by blogs, vlogs, or other spectacular things that haven't even been invented yet.

Diaries are great because they let you say WHAT you like WHEN you like. They are YOURS. They are not meant to be shared. They are just YOUR SPACE, where you can let it all out. I don't think there's a space on social media like it. As soon as we know we may have an audience, our attitude to what we are writing changes. This is mainly because none of us wants to be seen in a negative way. If we can help it, we don't want to let people see us at our most vulnerable or jealous or just downright nasty and angry. We all have these moments and that's why it's fantastically healthy to have a place to let all that gushing bile out. Diaries are a bucket to catch all your bad-feeling spew. You don't get judged, no one tries to "fix you," but you get to let it ALL out in complete safety. That's what I do, and it helps immensely.

Diaries can also be tremendously useful in therapy, to help you share with your therapist how you felt at a precise moment. Sometimes it's difficult to tell someone in an office how something felt at the time. A diary records that. It captures you and your feelings in a written space. I know some people like to do this by recording themselves on their phones. I'm not saying that's wrong, BUT again, LOOKING into a phone, LOOKING at yourself can take your brain to a different place. Even at my most distressed, my brain can notice my eyebrows are looking a bit scruffy—tragic but true. Diaries help to keep the focus.

They can also be a great way to track your recovery. That's what my old diaries do for me. I can see how far I've come from being seventeen. When you feel a bit better, you can look back on all the bad times and KNOW, to quote that great phrase, ALL THINGS MUST PASS. LOUSY times DO get better. That's a really comforting thought. It can give you a bit of mental armor for any hard times in the future. Once you know you can survive, you can do it again and again.

I still keep diaries for many reasons. Even dull days can be wonderful when you look back on them, and I guarantee in the past week a friend or family member has said something that's worth preserving for life. For example, the way my mum calls labradoodles "OodleDoodles" needs to be recorded for all eternity

Diaries capture YOUR moments—good, bad, and weird. They also give you an important safety valve. They let the volcano in your head explode before it goes FULL Pompeii. Sometimes people and situations still make me really angry. Sometimes this is fair. They are in the wrong. Sometimes I'm completely overreacting. Last week someone sent me an email. They should have called me. I RANTED for a good page and a half about how appalled I was, how other people were not treated like this, how

DISGUSTING it was, and then I read it back the next day and realized I was being utterly ridiculous. Crucially, though, I'd done no damage to a relationship, and only my lovely diary had heard me at my worst.

Keeping a diary means you get to share every part of you with something that will never tell your secrets, never expect you to be entertaining, never expect you to be "at your best." It just wants to listen and let YOU be YOU. If you're recovering or coping with a mental health condition, or you just want to keep mentally healthy, it's a great and inexpensive way to let everything inside of you OUT.

Get yourself some nice stationery (there's a lot of it about) and get writing.

Go to Sleep

Not now preferably. Read this first.

You cannot be healthy without sleep.
You need to sleep like you need to breathe.

Says the woman who binge-watches TV series until dawn and regularly gets caught down a YouTube hole at two in the morning. I'm the person who recently tweeted (at 3:05 A.M.) how annoying it was that I had to pee at 3 A.M. No one needed to know that. Let's not even talk about my Skype habits. Dreadful decisions. STUPID! Me and sleep. I do SO MUCH wrong and then I pay the price. To be honest, the people I live with and the people I work with pay the price too. Lack of sleep can cause you—

To have a total lack of concentration.

What was that last sentence I wrote?

Something. It was about . . .

To be a bit vague about stuff. You know. Stuff.

To be unable to control your moods. You make a slight mistake and you RAGE. RAGE. YES. YOU'VE RUN OUT OF MILK FOR YOUR CRANBERRY-AND-WHOLE-NUT MUESLI AND THIS IS THE ACTUAL BREAKFAST APOCALYPSE RIGHT NOW.

To cry at anything. Not the usual things—weird stuff. Packages, Lego, pavement.

To be irritable beyond belief.

To have a desperate need to eat cookies constantly.

To feel sad.

To laugh at nothing.

Isn't that fence funny?

Probably not.

I'm speaking from experience.

The issue is, the world has never been so distracting. Our phones are a real temptation. They are bursting at the seams with people to talk to, and things to see and watch, and beeps and alerts. The world never sleeps, and we can be awake with it.

The problem is, your brain doesn't care about that. It needs sleep. It always has. The amount it needs will differ from person to person, but we all need a certain amount. And as well as distracting us, our phones may also be preventing us from getting to sleep.

> **Dr. R. says:** *Phone, or "blue," light affects melatonin, the hormone that makes us sleepy and controls our sleep-wake cycle, so phone use just before bed can disrupt the quality and quantity of our sleep.*

Basically, most of us could probably do with less screen time. But it's very difficult to break the phone habit.

This has been a BIG step for me, but honestly, here's what I've had to start doing.

I leave the phone in another room.

Forgive me if I sound pathetic, I do not for one minute think this is a huge act of bravery, but it has been huge for me. I had to do it in stages. Just outside the door the first night, and then eventually IN. THE. LIVING ROOM. I kept reaching over to get it. It wasn't there. Momentary panic. Then I reminded myself:

People will find me if there really is an emergency. I don't need to tell everyone I can't sleep on Twitter. A really nice photo of my new peacock duvet cover for Instagram can wait until the morning.

It Can All Wait for Sleep

I figure as long as I've got a smoke alarm, I don't really need any other devices around me. I didn't have a smartphone for years. I don't need one now.

If you're using your phone as your alarm, get an alarm clock. And get your phone outside your bedroom.

Of course, lack of sleep isn't just caused by mobile phones. Insomnia has been a problem since long before social media. It can be a symptom of mental illness, or an underlying medical condition. If you are having trouble sleeping because you're worried or your brain won't turn off or you just never seem to feel tired, do see your doctor. It might be that you've got into a bad sleep pattern and you need some help to get into a good one. There are even sleep clinics that can help you. Your doctor, if they feel it is appropriate, can put you in touch with these.

Your brain wants to be unconscious for at least some of the day so it can repair itself and you. Let it be. When you go to bed, put your brain to bed too. Tuck it up and tell it a story. Do not let it watch *Top of the Pops* from 1996, binge-watch *Stranger Things*, and then get into a Twitter fight.

There are many great ways to keep your head healthy. Exercise, meditation, taking quiz shows like *Jeopardy!* RE-ALLY seriously and learning facts for them—all these things help to keep me well. The key is to find what works for YOU and to keep doing it—even on days when you don't really feel like it (opposite action at work again!).

Mental Health and Extraordinary Times

By "extraordinary times" I mean when there are generally heightened levels of emotion among just about everyone.

These can be split into two main categories.

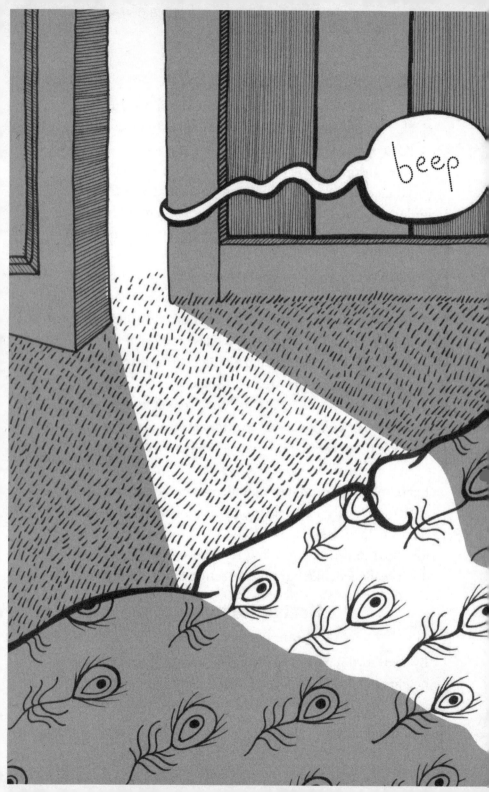

The first:

Times When Everyone Expects You to Be Happy Because "Yay! Celebration Thing Is Happening" and You're Feeling Not So Good

OK, I'm mainly talking about the holiday season.

Not just the holidays, though. I'm also talking about all those times when everyone else seems like they are bouncing about in joy—birthdays, anniversaries, New Year's Eve, or driving-test passes after four attempts. Sometimes we can plan for these occasions, and sometimes they are more unexpected.

I celebrate Christmas, so I'll use Christmas as the example. We know it's coming every year and, whatever belief you have, you can't really escape it. Christmas is like a magnifying glass for feelings. If you're feeling great, you'll feel like all the tinsel and the glitter makes everything even more wonderful. However, if you're not feeling well, it can also magnify that too.

Feeling unhappy when everything around you is telling you YOU SHOULD feel happy is very difficult. It's a real pressure. It can make you feel like joy is being forced onto you, which in turn can make you feel incredibly isolated. The trick is to remember that, at extraordinary times, you have the ability to stay ordinary.

Christmas, for example, isn't compulsory. If it's all getting too much, you can politely back down a tad from everything. This doesn't have to be in anger so it spoils everyone else's day. You just need to give yourself a break for a bit to get away from it all. If you don't want to explain, tell people you've got a terrible headache and you need to lie down for half an hour. This will give you some peace from the sensory OVERLOAD.

Extraordinary events can happen at any time of year. Have a safe place. If your home is too noisy, or has too much conflict in it, arrange somewhere you can go where it's quiet and you don't have to join in. This could be a library, a park, a friend's bedroom, or a field. It's just finding a place where you can get away from the world so when you return to everyone else you'll be in a better state to enjoy/cope with the situation on your own terms.

Second category:

Times When Everyone Seems Stressed/ Scared/Angry/Worried

This can mean times when the world seems scary and people around you are anxious. But the world has always had its deeply worrying parts, and the education system has always had EXAMS. You need to develop ways of coping with this.

If the people around you are getting stressed and it's making you stressed, remove yourself from the conversation or the social media discussion. Sometimes going over and over things you have no control of makes you feel worse, not better. For example, comparing homework planners may be unhelpful for you. If it is, go and do some studying or something you find relaxing.

Try to separate your head from what is happening everywhere else. We all process things at different speeds. Give yourself the time YOU need to get your head around things.

To summarize keeping your head healthy:

Remember that
you're more than a mental
illness. You are not just your
diagnosis. You don't have to wear
it and share it unless you want to.
It's not your duty.

The world is
triggering. Give yourself the
power to cope with those triggers
or remove yourself from those
situations until you can
cope with them.

Keeping your
phone on all night is like
keeping a baby awake all
night deliberately.
Eventually it will
lead to disaster.

Put your phone
away every night. Make it a
small bed if you like so it can
charge and rest in peace and quiet.
It has needs too, you know. (You
don't have to read it a story, but
you can if you like.)

Get some sleep.
A big, huge chunk.
Perferably eight hours
or more, regularly.

Find some
safe places where
you can escape to
if necessary.

GIVE YOURSELF A BREAK.
I can't say that enough,
so I'm going to keep
on saying it.

"I've got a really beautifully shaped lobe"

Keeping Your Head Healthy with the Ten-Minute Head Gym

When people ask me if I go to the gym, I can honestly answer yes. My gym is the finest in the land. There's no membership fee. It doesn't involve paying a HUGE monthly bill. Neither will you have to put up with big muscly guys going, "URGGGHHHHH!" as they lift enormous weights and sweat a lot. The only straggly armpit hair you will see in my gym is your own.

I have a head gym, it's free, and you can join from wherever you are. You don't have to be feeling bad to do it, and it's a great start to the morning. It's an easy three-step routine.

 Sit or lie down somewhere quiet and put your phone out of the way. Breathe deeply in, out, and in for five minutes using the Kirby Method™ (see pages 50–51). As you do this, chant to yourself in your head, "Dear Brain. You are brilliant. You can handle this day." Your brain is listening and will take this statement on board if you repeat it enough. It is the truth. It just needs to hear it.

After doing this for five minutes (it will seem like ages and you may feel a bit stupid at

184

first, but it's SO worth it), find a song you can go completely crazy to. Go somewhere private and LOSE YOURSELF IN THE BEAUTY OF THE GROOVE. There are some suggestions for tunes in my "Dr. Pop" section at the back of the book, but you can use ANYTHING. If the theme tune to *The Big Bang Theory* makes you want to move, use that. It doesn't matter. The combination of music and dance will release all sorts of joyous chemical wonder in your brain and body.

3 Following this, stand on your tiptoes, stretch your hands up in the air, and ROAR or YELL or SHOUT "YES!" This was a top tip given to me by a very successful friend. I thought she'd gone a bit too far at first, BUT it really works. It's like an ancient war cry! If you've ever watched *Braveheart*, the Scots do it before they fight King Edward's vastly better-equipped army with basically sharpened logs, and win. There's something quite cavewoman/caveman about it too. Try it. It makes you feel POWERFUL.

As with all my suggestions, please tweak the mind gym to suit you. I pick up tips from people all over the place. If someone suggests something (and it's not dangerous), I try it. What's the worst that could happen? If it's looking and sounding like a bit of an ass, I can totally live with that.

BE YOUR OWN GREATEST FAN

Self-esteem and How to Get It

What Is Self-Esteem?

Self-esteem is basically fangirling/fanboying yourself on a constant basis without even really knowing it. It's giving yourself some serious love and confidence. It's an arm around your own shoulder constantly saying, "You're doing OK." It's believing that you've got a lot to offer the world. Sometimes it can feel like a trumpet fanfare. Sometimes it's quiet and still and deep inside you. It's very forgiving too. It tells you when you've done something wrong, but it doesn't obsess about it or punish you for it.

From where I'm working, I can see a new housing complex being built. And I've noticed the builders spend ages on the foundations. Ages. There's concrete, there are big poles and thick iron. The builders are getting levels out every five minutes and checking stuff. It seems to take months and involves lots of chats and cups of tea. Self-esteem is the same. It's like having a brilliantly strong foundation inside you that the rest of your brain home gets built on.

Which is all very well, but how the hell do you build a house without plans? I mean, no one tells you this stuff. How do you get self-esteem? I've googled self-esteem architects and they don't exist. That's because it's up to you to build self-esteem. You don't need a hard hat or a high-visibility jacket. You just need some time. Here are some ways to get the construction process started:

Your Brain Is Listening, So Speak Nicely to It, Please

Your whole head is a sophisticated surveillance device. It's got twenty-four-hour CCTV and a voice recorder running ALL the time. It's got ears bigger than an elephant and the appetite of another . . . elephant. They say elephants have good memories too. YOUR BRAIN IS BASICALLY THE WORLD'S SMARTEST ELEPHANT.

So stop telling your elephant it is small and insignificant. It is not. Speak kindly to your elephant. Give it lots of encouragement and positive reinforcement. Your brain is listening. It's taking detailed notes. There's an old saying: "What we say we are is what we become." So big yourself up, as opposed to putting yourself down. You wouldn't speak to a friend that way, so why speak to yourself that way?!

You need to practice speaking to yourself as though you are another person. A good place to practice is in a mirror. YES—you will feel stupid and may cringe at first, BUT it's a really simple thing to do. Sit in front of the mirror and say, "INSERT OWN NAME HERE, you are brilliant. You are unique. You are loved and this world needs you." Say it over and over. The elephant in your brain will be listening, and it will begin to believe it. Your self-esteem will go from a small, cowering baby elephant to a huge proud one that can charge at ivory poachers. Sorry. Probably stretched the whole elephant thing too far. But what I'm saying is that GOOD self-esteem and a solid sense of self-worth can protect us from some of life's pitfalls, and that can only be a good thing.

Perfection Does Not Exist. Imperfection Is Perfection.

If you want good self-esteem, give up the idea that perfection exists. Nothing is perfect except for giant anteaters. You're never going to be one of those.

No one looks perfect. Supermodels have bad hair days. Beautiful, groomed celebrities fart and get bloated. Pictures are airbrushed and filtered. Perfection has to be created. In real life, IN REALITY, there is no such thing.

No one is perfect. The nicest person has nasty moments. The smartest person has knowledge gaps. "Beautiful" people have flaws. Perfection does not exist.

If you set yourself the unobtainable target of perfection, you are basically telling yourself you don't deserve to be happy. Even in sports where perfect scores exist, once that perfection is attained someone creates another perfection that's even better (see Olympic gymnastics from 1976 onward).

Perfection does not exist.

Good self-esteem should not be waiting for a time when you are perfect. You deserve to feel good about yourself today. Set yourself manageable daily targets. By all means stretch yourself. Aim high.

Aim the highest you think you can possibly attain, but if you fall short, don't allow that to cripple you. Self-esteem also shouldn't be based on external things and opinions. It's more than that. This is why some athletes really struggle after they stop competing. All their life, "feeling good" has been based on their results. That's a wonderful validation of their efforts, but it actually isn't "them." So once they stop competing, they have to learn new ways to build their self-esteem.

Start living now. John Lennon said, "Life is what happens to you while you're busy making other plans." The best way to build your self-esteem is to enjoy your life NOW and the skills you have NOW. If that seems impossible because you don't like yourself NOW, you first need to give up the idea of perfection, and then read the rest of this chapter.

Unless you're reading this and you're a giant anteater. In which case you've got no excuse. You've got legs shaped like furry pants, a massive tongue, AND you can read. What's your problem?!

For the rest of us non-anteaters, perfection does not happen. Aim high, but don't build your self-esteem on the shaky sand of something that doesn't really exist.

Celebrate All Your Achievements

When you do something great, do something for yourself. Your self-esteem needs to be reminded! This doesn't have to be anything expensive. It doesn't even have to be a "thing." It can be a really long bath with some excellent music or a podcast and a candle. It can be whatever you enjoy. As I've said before, there's no such thing as a guilty pleasure. If it's not hurting you and it's not hurting anyone else, do what the hell you like to make you feel good. If that means watching *SpongeBob Squarepants* even though you are over the age of seven, that is absolutely fine. Your self-esteem loves a bit of fun and a reminder that you deserve to be treated well.

Get Earplugs When Idiots Are About

No one is responsible for building your self-esteem, but no one has the right to make you feel lousy about yourself either. It's your responsibility to defend yourself against that. If you have got people around you being negative, tune them out. If you can't lose them from your life altogether, then develop selective deafness when they are around. If this is happening on social media, use the mute and block functions—not just the actual ones that these platforms have, but try to develop some in your head too.

It's also important to have a tough-love army around you. These are people that you trust completely and that can tell it to you straight but with total kindness and with your best interests at heart. Hopefully this is your family and friends, but it could also be someone at school, someone you work with, or someone from one of the organizations listed at the back of this book.

Having good people around you is essential for good mental health. Get yourself a team that supports you. You're not expecting them to do all the hard work for you—you just don't want them to knock down the foundations you are trying to build. Kind, supportive friends can make all the difference in a person's life. It's not the quantity either—it's the quality of these friends that makes the difference.

Comparing Yourself to Others
Never Helps Your Self-esteem

AMAZING FACT! You are YOU! You are a one-off special-edition collector's item limited run of one—ONE-OFF, UNIQUE-IN-THE-HISTORY-OF-THE-WORLD YOU.

So why are you comparing yourself to anyone else?

We all do it—for years and years I'd look around and compare myself to everyone else. Why wasn't I thinner, quieter, sexier? I used to look at models and wonder why I couldn't be like them! SEX BOMBS. REAL women. I guarantee people look at Kylie Jenner now and think exactly the same thing.

But all that time I was comparing myself to those women in magazines I was ignoring the amazing parts of me.

Trust me, so many bits of you are brilliant RIGHT NOW. But, as I write, you may be missing them because you're looking at or thinking about someone else that you've decided is better than you. Unless you are looking at or thinking about Beyoncé, Barack Obama, or Elizabeth I, YOU ARE WRONG.

First Thing to Do:

Write down all the things that are wonderful about you. This is HARD. We're often not encouraged to believe things like "I am hugely clever" or "I am funny." If you're having trouble doing this, perhaps you feel that it sounds a bit bigheaded or arrogant. It's not. It's simply appreciating YOU, and that's an essential part of being mentally healthy.

My best friend, Mort, helped me to appreciate me. She reminded me I am, among a few things, unbelievable at trivia quizzes. Plus I can sing every TV theme EVER perfectly WORD FOR WORD (even the ones that have no words). I'd taken my memory for granted, but being a treasured member of a quiz team still makes me feel great.

Ask a friend, a parent, a relative, a teacher, or anyone who knows you well, "What do you think is good about me?" Sometimes it's very difficult to look in the mirror

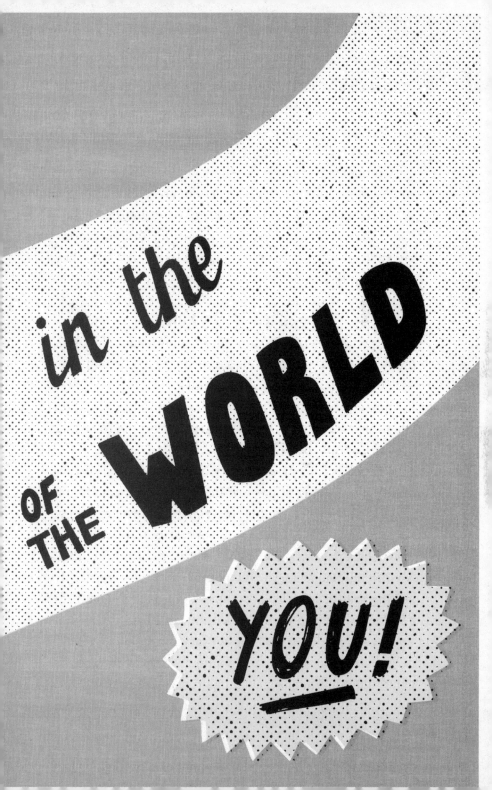

and get an accurate reflection back. Asking other people what they appreciate and value about YOU may give you some surprising and rewarding answers. The combination of answers will be as unique as you are.

Comparing yourself to others is also useless because you have no idea what other people are going through. What they present to the world may not be the reality. People have a face they show to the world. You're comparing yourself to what people want you to see, not who they actually fully are.

Failure Is So Fine

Some people let failure dent their self-esteem. This is ridiculous. Massive-enormous-ass mistakes are actually the very foundation of great self-esteem.

Some people are so frightened of failure they don't do what they want to do. This is a very quick route to feeling dreadful about yourself.

Failure is fine. It is NOTHING to be scared of (unless you are failing at performing a very high trapeze act without a safety net). Failure just proves that you're trying. As long as you learn from your mistakes and don't keep repeating a pattern of behavior, failure is a beautiful thing. My life has been beset with cock-ups that have inevitably led to great things JUST because I got back up again. If you know you can come back from an EPIC FAIL, you know you can defeat just about everything.

Failure is how we learn. Failure is how we get stronger. Failure is how we get things right. You KNOW this. You KNOW the stories. J. K. Rowling was a single mom on the poverty line. She described herself as a failure. SHE ENDED UP WRITING *HARRY POTTER*. Bill Gates dropped out of school but became the world's youngest self-made billionaire. Steven Spielberg got bad grades in school and was rejected from his dream school, UCLA. He's got TWO BEST DIRECTOR OSCARS, a TON of Oscar nominations, and has made more than fifty (mainly brilliant) films.

Even when the stakes are HUGE, it's fine to fail. It's fine to admit you've failed. We all do it, and people love you for admitting it.

AS LONG AS YOU WORK TO COME BACK FROM IT, IT'S FINE.

Also, please stop labeling things as failure. It's such a loaded word. Your brain is listening all the time. Failure is actually the triumph of doing something rather than nothing. You can survive failure. What you can't survive is not making the best of magnificent brilliant you. Accept that failure is a part of becoming the best you can be; accept it's a part of life. It won't kill you off. It'll make you stronger.

Sorry—I sound like a meme again, but I mean it.

You're a Bit of an Idiot. That's Normal. Everyone Is. That's Fine Too.

You're an idiot. That's OK. We all are. All of us have things about ourselves that we can't change. They are inherent to us and help to make our personality. We also all have weaknesses and things about ourselves that we don't really like. I am loud and chatty. Especially when I'm nervous. A national newspaper once called me bumptious, which means "arrogantly overassertive." I am never going to walk into a room and be the graceful, quiet type.

I used to hate myself for this until my husband (strong introvert type) pointed out that if I were a man I'd be called charismatic, not bumptious, and that he loved the way I was with people.

And that's true. So I decided to own it.

And actually I can turn it into a positive thing at parties. I am quite good at bringing a room together and getting people chatting. On the flip side, I do sometimes feel socially responsible for everyone in the world ever (THAT is being bumptious), but I try not to dwell on that. The point is, a weakness can also be a strength. And even if your weakness is just a weakness, THAT IS FINE. I am the world's clumsiest person. It is not cute. We go through about twelve new mugs a year. That's a weakness, but I'm human. Good self-esteem comes from accepting who we are and everything that we are, crap bits and all.

Not being the best at everything lets other people shine too. Let other people be good at the things you're not so good at. I am the world's worst driver. It took me seven years to pass my test. Seriously, I nearly finished off an IKEA superstore once. Consequently my husband drives everywhere. He quite enjoys the fact that he gets to do this for me, and I get to enjoy the fact that I am not seriously injuring a sofa called "Goteborg" and/or another human being. Let other people come into your life and show you what they can do. Don't compare or be sad that you haven't got a particular natural skill—admire in others what you don't have in yourself. I think if we all just pooled our resources, this world would run so much more smoothly.

Being bad at things is fine. Besides, my husband is awful at trivia quizzes.

Help Yourself by Helping Others

It's worth repeating that a great way to feel better about yourself is to feel useful. You can actually help yourself by helping others. It doesn't have to be helping humans either. If other people seem too daunting to you, try volunteering at an animal shelter. Working with animals can be a great way to build self-confidence and self-worth. They give back to you in a lovely way, not through words but often by something more magical.

Try volunteering at different places. It can really help you to work out where your skills and talents truly lie. One of the turning points in my life was volunteering to go to Poland to teach English. Seeing that I could be (a) OK in another country and (b) actually good and able in a really-quite-responsible teaching job made me feel AMAZING. Plus there is now a whole generation of Polish people who, thanks to me, can do the hokey pokey. I went from being somebody who really didn't like who they were to somebody who really appreciated the odd bits about themselves.

When you help others you help yourself. It's something worth way more than money. Even a few hours a week can make all the difference.

"ONLY TWO LIKES?! I AM A MONSTER!"

Social Media

I know I've touched on social media elsewhere in this book, but I wanted to give it a chapter on its own. It's an important part of most of our lives and it's still a relatively new world. A new world that has made the generations act a bit . . . differently.

Once upon a time, older people used to know the answer to just about everything. They were wise. Basically everything you'd done they'd done, just in black-and-white photos. You could ask them how they'd coped with stuff. Some things were very different, but relationships/dating/communication were basically the same as they always had been. Older people could really help.

And then the internet came along and everything changed. Old people started asking younger people for help with googling. The world began to move at a pace they just couldn't keep up with. And THEN social media happened and things went crazy. People like my mom got Facebook, and her status updates were all about having poached eggs for breakfast and how Nigel the taxi driver was picking her up to meet Pauline at Sainsbury's for soup and a roll.

She writes everything on Facebook. "Just read paper. My sunflower is growing" was another one. OVERSHARE, Mom—but she doesn't know what that means!

Social media is a whole new world for ALL of us, and young people are leading the way. Innovators will make mistakes. The key is to try not to make the mistakes really huge ones.

There is no doubt you'll be far savvier on social media than I ever will be. I can't work out Snapchat. I've tried because I want to make my face into a puppy, but it's not happening. Tumblr is magnificent, but I'm confused. The art on there is astounding, but . . .

Perhaps I might be getting . . . . . . old.

Anyway, it doesn't really matter what the platform is. How you handle yourself on any social media is the key thing. Here are just a few things to keep in mind. These are some of the rules I play by. I've learned the hard way too, so please don't think this advice hasn't come about via some classic mistakes, because it has.

What to Share

Even with the most locked-down settings in the history of the internet, social media is your online tattoo. Everything you write or every photo you share will probably be read or seen by someone. It can be screen-grabbed, even if you delete it. It can stay in people's memories too. If you share it, it's there. It becomes "real" to other people. That's the joy of it, though, isn't it? It's lovely to be able to tell loads of people ALL AT ONCE about the good stuff that's happening in your life.

A good question to ask yourself is WHY you are sharing something. If you've had an excellent night with your friends and you want to spread the love and joy—great. If you want to share something you've created because you're proud of it—wonderful. If you want to vlog about something you feel passionate about (like planes, for example . . .) feel FREE! If you've had a great burrito and you want to take a picture of it—fine. I'm with you. Excellent. Delicious Mexican food *should* go viral. Everything will get a reaction. Even vlogs about railway level crossings get a reaction. But are you ready for that reaction? Always remember you don't have to read the comments and the "disable comments" function available on some platforms is there for a REASON. The tougher decisions come when you are sharing the more intimate stuff in your life.

If you're feeling vulnerable or sad, you may want to

tell everyone too, but why? Is it going to make you feel better? What's the real reason for creating the post? Are you trying to get sympathy or love? Totally understandable. But perhaps calling or hugging a friend would be a better option, and much more satisfying for you. Anger is another thing you need to be careful with. If you're angry, take a deep breath and RANT and RAVE on an email

or on paper. SAY WHAT YOU LIKE! But don't put the address or name on it. Leave it as a draft and then walk away from it. Sleep on it. If you still feel the same way the next day (and you may be completely right to be angry), you'll probably be able to be more controlled about things. Anger is at its most effective when it's controlled and directed at the right person.

Tantrums don't work well in real life if you're over the age of three, but they look even worse written down. People love the drama of anger too. It's the sort of stuff they enjoy sharing. You don't want your peak moment of (perhaps really righteous) fury to become something people laugh at. Whenever you share something online, try to imagine getting into the TARDIS and seeing your posts in five years' time. Life changes quickly. Do you really want to commit this feeling or thought to something that potentially could be around forever and ever and ever? I'm happy to tell you now that I love vegetarian nachos. This will never change. Let guacamole be inscribed on my gravestone as the greatest thing ever except for my son, music, and anteaters. All other things are open to debate. Even things we think are certain change. This isn't because you are young. This is because it's life, and change will definitely happen throughout it. Every time you share, just ask yourself WHY you're really doing it.

Sexting

Sexting is sending sexual stuff over the phone. It could be messages, photos, or videos. In many parts of the world, it's illegal to do this under the age of eighteen.

Even if it is legal where you are, *please* think seriously before you sext anything. Pictures and messages can be shared very easily these days, and devices can be hacked. You don't want something meant for one person to end up being looked at by loads of people. If a partner is pressuring you to do something you don't want to, tell them to get lost. If someone loves you, they can remember what your body looks like without a photo. They can hear you say things that are sexy without you sending them. You don't have to record it or write it all down. That's why we have imaginations. If someone really respects you, they will understand that you don't want to share. You're not a vacation resort—you don't have to give out souvenirs.

> **Dr. R. says:** *Always think a million times before sending an image like this, of yourself or anyone else, to ANYONE. If someone is pressuring you or asking you to do anything you are not comfortable with or to send anything you would not feel happy showing your grandma, then DON'T DO IT! There are some great apps that can help you send back a funny NO to a request for someone hassling you. Zipit from Childline is one. Once that image is out there, it is no longer in your control, and you could be bullied or blackmailed. If you are worried because someone is asking you to share an image, then tell a friend or an adult you trust who can support you in this.*

Who and What to Believe Online

It's easy for anyone to create a completely fake person to draw someone into their world. I have conversations on Twitter all the time with people I've never met or spoken to. I assume they are the person in the photo, but are they really? It doesn't matter so much if I'm just swapping my views on TV shows about cakes, but what are the implications of building friendships/relationships? Basically, unless you are talking to someone you know and have met in real life, you've got to turn into a complete Sherlock if you're having an online friendship. Going full detective is vital.

Examine all their accounts in minute detail. How many friends do they have? If you google them, what comes up? Are they vague about details but expect you to share a lot? Do a reverse Google image search. Don't take ANYTHING anyone says at face value.

It comes down to one simple question:

What Does This Person Really Want Me to Believe and Why?

Exactly the same thing applies to global news. Is what I'm reading actually true? It may LOOK true, but IS IT true? Who has created this news? What does that person want from me? Do they want me to believe their version of things so I support them? Why do they want me to support them? What does supporting them mean? Why do they want to influence my brain?

Social media news is not policed. There is nothing to stop me from going on Twitter now and saying, "A woman with short blond hair just stole my purse! That's the third one this week! Sad!" If I want you to feel suspicious of women with short blond hair, that's a great way to start. Get your news from a wide variety of sources and make your own mind up.

Cyberbullying

When it comes to cyberbullying, I have a theory. You can think about why the cyberbully is doing it and drive yourself slightly crazy in the process. You can wonder why they're saying dreadful things to you or telling lies about you, but in the end you will probably never know. Perhaps *they* will never know. There are a million reasons why someone might bully someone else. Your cyberbully may be someone you've never met, someone you know or someone you have known. It's a very human feeling to want to understand why someone does mean things to you, but a lot of the time the person doing it isn't quite sure either. If you spend a lot of your time wondering WHY someone is acting the way they are, you are doing their therapy for them.

The effect on you may be very, very hurtful. I think a lot of us have suffered attacks online. Older people may say things like, "You shouldn't let this bother you" or "Words cannot really hurt you." In one sense they have a point—words are just words and, to some extent, we choose what effect they have on us. If someone on Twitter calls me an "ugly, fat bitch," I can live with that. It causes me no grief whatsoever. It's probably some eleven-year-old . . . why even speculate? That's not fair to eleven-year-olds. Just park any theories you may have and move on. Go and talk to a friend, speak to someone lovely, and "block" the offender. What someone "yells" on social media is NOT reality. Your time is better spent with the positive people in your life.

However, if the attacks continue over days, weeks, and months, and over different social media sites, it's far harder to deal with emotionally. People can be VILE. It used to be that you could physically avoid bullies and what they said to you. (I had special routes to get to my house from school to avoid them.) Your home and your bedroom were a place of safety. Now bullies live in the palm of your hand, but why should YOU give up social media? If you've done nothing wrong, why should you be bullied off?

Keep a diary of everything that goes on. Screen-grab and file it away so you don't have to look at it but you have a record of it. Tell someone you trust about it. If the harassment continues, or if you are ever concerned about your safety, contact the police.

What I wouldn't do is communicate with the bully. They may try a whole range of tactics to try and get you to engage with them—from saying really nasty stuff, to appearing to be reasonable, to contacting your friends. Whatever they do, don't feed the beast. Don't put up with it either. Talk to someone in authority about it and show them what's been happening. They can help you to cope with it and work out ways to get it to stop.

Trolls

Sadly we live in an age where some people are rewarded for being as controversial as possible. My theory is, there are so many opinions and so much noise that people tend to SHOUT SOMETHING OUTRAGEOUS AS LOUD AS POSSIBLE to get noticed. For example, no one will take notice of the tweet "The squirrels stealing the bird food in my garden are annoying me," BUT if I wrote "ALL SQUIRRELS DESERVE A PUNCH IN THEIR FURRY STUPID FACES!!!"* people would take notice.

I think you have to be a really strong person to cope with and engage with trolls on a regular basis. You need both the tools and the time. That's a BIG ASK. You have to be either a professional stand-up comedian who is used to dealing with hecklers and demolishes trolls online wittily, or someone who is used to dealing with huge amounts of grief. For many celebrities, it sadly comes with the job. James Blunt does it really well. He's someone with so much self-belief and confidence that he can be self-deprecating and burn someone at the same time. I don't really like the guy's music, but he's magnificent on Twitter. It's about deciding what your limits are. Me? I just mute/block/ignore. My Twitter page is my view. If you want to argue with me in a civilized fashion—cool. I might chat back. I might not. That's your prerogative too. You don't have to respond to everyone who gets in touch with you. You don't

---

* I love squirrels. Don't hurt them. They are like pigeons. Just surviving. Just doing their thing. I've lots of respect for so-called vermin in general, actually.

have to respond to every world event. When I get trolled, I just mute the trolls. For someone like me, it's the sensible choice. Work out your limits on each platform. And don't be afraid to leave a troll yelling in the dark. Real trolls live under bridges. They're used to it.

When Things Go Bad

There used to be a saying, "Today's news is tomorrow's wastepaper," which meant that when someone did something terrible that made the newspaper, the next day that newspaper was in the bin. Now things that go bad tend to stick around for longer and can be shared far more widely far more quickly, but . . . I still believe that the "wastepaper" principle kind of works because of what I said earlier—we are all idiots. If you do something stupid today, someone else will do something stupid within the next hour. If something dumb you've done does go viral, apologize if you need to and then come offline for a while. Someone else stupid will come along and cancel out everyone talking about your stupid thing.

Perhaps we all just need to be a bit more forgiving of sudden acts of silly too. I DO NOT mean go soft on people who are genuinely hurting others or professional trolls or criminals. I mean if someone who is normally basically sound does something dumb, let's call them an idiot but not ALL pile on them baying for blood.

Likewise, let's not share cruel memes or photos that make fun of ordinary people. That's someone's family member/friend. If you see someone who's tired/drunk/

emotional/in distress, try to stop anyone with you from taking a video or a photo.

Had somebody been recording the main road where I caught the bus the other morning, there would currently be a video called "Epic Run for the Bus FAIL!" My tumble was spectacular, and it was in front of an entire traffic jam. I flew through the air with such height and force that I had time to think, "This is going to hurt and look stupid"—and it did. Luckily a woman pulled over to check that I was OK. I was. Although my tracksuit bottoms were ripped, my knee was shredded, my pride was dented, AND still I missed the bloody bus. Seriously, that was bad enough without the whole world getting a laugh from it.

It sounds a bit glib and simple, but let's just be kinder to people who make mistakes, people who do the odd dumb thing, and people who fall over running to catch the bus.

It's Time to Switch Off from Social Media When . . .

Your phone is replacing everything else in your life. Social media is a great way to get in touch with people, but it doesn't replace actually being with and talking to people. I don't necessarily mean socializing in a big group or going to parties. For a lot of us that isn't our scene. I mean talking to friends face-to-face. Doing stuff with friends where you may have your phone on you, but your phone isn't the main activity. Phones should be a mainly solitary activity. Other humans might enjoy your time, lots of eye contact, and a period away from social media. Your phone is a bit of a taker in your life. Don't miss out on something because you are watching a video of a panda sneezing. (I speak from experience obviously.)

You're not getting enough sleep. As we've said, sleep is one of the single biggest things you can do for your brain, and for your physical and mental health in general. Go to sleep. Switch off. Turn the phone off.

You're obsessing about your appearance online. We all like to look our best in photos, but if you are taking twenty-plus to get one selfie, there's a problem. It's a waste of time and it says you're uncomfortable with how you look. Remember, perfection doesn't exist. The amazing photos you see in magazines take HOURS to create. Someone in Los Angeles did my makeup once and I looked twenty years younger. There's a reason why they are called makeup ARTISTS. It's unbelievable what they can do. If you had access to that every day, you would look permanently fresh-faced and "spectacular," but it's not real. Set yourself a three-selfie rule. Three selfies MAX and then choose the best one. The world can take you as you are—imperfectly perfect.

You're obsessing about getting likes. Your life is not a brand, like McDonald's or Nike. You don't have to organize focus groups to find out what people think about you and the things that you post. Big companies spend millions to research why the public likes things. This is because people are fickle and unpredictable. They get up at different times and go to bed at different times. They might not see what you've posted. Their pet goldfish may have just died and they are not in the mood to respond. An alien spacecraft may have abducted them. Why worry? You can't base your self-esteem on other people. Other people are just too weird. You cannot hand over control of one of the most important things in your life—your self-worth—to something so random. It's a recipe for misery. The true innovators and creators in life do their thing and then walk away. I doubt David Bowie ever lost sleep over the number of likes he got. I try to remember that every time a tweet that I think is brilliant completely tanks.

You are viewing real life through your phone. Everyone loves a good picture on Instagram. I took a magnificent shot of a rose covered in raindrops on the way to my son's school once (go and have a look—EPIC). It's still there. Beautiful. But I also took time to SMELL the aforementioned rose and appreciate its beauty on my own. Take great photos—they are wonderful to look at. But don't put your entire life through a lens. If you see something beautiful, don't instantly grab your phone. If you don't manage to get a shot of it, it's not the end of the world. It's in your head giving you pleasure. The rest of us will manage. There is lots to look at.

When it's upsetting you, get off. As previously stated, unless you're a world leader, no one is waiting for your opinion.

"BUT I REALLY LOVE YOU"

Sex and Relationships

This isn't a sex education book, but sex, relationships, and love are all magnificent and the MOST POTENTIALLY COMPLICATED AND CONFUSING PARTS OF LIFE EVER. Especially when you are looking after your brain.

So . . . love and sex and all that. I'll try to keep it simple.

Questions to Ask Yourself Before Having Sex:

1. Do I Really Want to Do This?

If you do, GREAT. If you don't, don't. Just don't. Even if you've said yes, you're allowed to change your mind. No means no.

Seriously, though, do you really want to do this?

Do you? I'm not being your mom by the way. Do what you like, but don't be bullied/persuaded into something you're not sure about.

It doesn't matter what age you are.

2. Am I Really Ready for This?

Are you? Is this the right time? There's a reason why the age of consent in many places is sixteen years old or even older. Sex brings complications with it. It's an emotionally demanding thing even if it feels light and frothy. Have you got contraception?

Do I sound like your grandma? Don't care. I'm trying to stop major-life-disaster stuff.

3. Am I Doing This for the Right Reasons?

Losing your virginity isn't a race. Sex isn't a competition. Only do it if YOU want to do it.

4. Am I Doing This to Please Someone Else/ Because Someone Else Wants To?

If you are, just DON'T.

In all of us, there is a little voice called instinct that sometimes yells at us to do something or not do something. If that little voice is yelling at you that something is wrong, it's silly to ignore it. If a situation or person just doesn't feel right, chances are it isn't, and they are not. When you have sex is YOUR choice and should be based on when you're really ready. When in doubt—wait. I wish

I had on a few occasions. Being dumped after having sex on a golf course in November and lending him TWENTY DOLLARS was lousy, for example. My point is, sex isn't going anywhere. It's how the human race continues. You won't miss out by waiting.

Mistakes will happen and that's fine too. Strength comes from learning from these mistakes, bouncing back, and moving forward.

You're Not Perfect. Neither Will Sex Be.

A lot of people think they don't deserve a relationship because they don't feel physically good enough. They feel they aren't thin enough or pretty enough or that certain parts of them should be bigger or smaller. This isn't a new problem or one that necessarily stops when you get older.

So, YOU have to remind yourself that this is nonsense.

There's an old Eddie Murphy sketch where he points out that everyone is ugly when they are having sex because they make stupid faces. This is true. Also those folds of skin you have that you don't like actually stop you from snapping in half when you stretch. You don't have to be perfect to have sex, and sex will not be perfect. There's always fumbling about, bits of your body that you may never truly like, bodies make strange noises—it's all natural. And basically everyone has a weird orgasm face. The key is to have sex with someone who you like, who likes you, and who you can have a laugh with. In my experience, intimate things like sex work better when you have existing intimacy and trust with someone.

Boyfriends and Girlfriends Don't Make You Better. Don't Expect Them To.

Sadly you cannot sex your way to self-esteem. This is a mistake a lot of us make.

I made it. I was feeling lousy about myself once, so I accepted the first man who showed any interest in me. I thought, "This man (actually any man) will make me feel spectacular about myself. I will be adored. I will be loved. Because I am loved I will love myself."

This did not happen.

Cue far too long being with probably the most unsuitable man for me on this earth. He just didn't seem to like me. Everything I did was wrong. I was too loud, too funny (!!), didn't have sex enough, and, most tragically of all, I ate pickled onions wrong. How can you eat pickled onions wrong? I've just asked my husband. He says, "You can't—unless you're choking on them." That's the right answer.

The point is, every tiny thing I did to/with this boyfriend annoyed him. Breathing. I'm not joking. I did that too loudly.

My self-esteem did not rocket with this person. It plummeted even further. By the end of the relationship, I believed him when he said, "You'll never find anyone else to put up with you." I thought, "That's fine! I will be single forever. It's better that way."

It was HIS problem he was an ass, but it was mine that I had made one fundamental error.

I had expected a relationship with someone else to fix my relationship with myself. It couldn't. He couldn't. No one could.

The problem is, when you don't like yourself, you can make very bad choices. You may even attract the kind of person who improves their own self-esteem by making other people feel lousy. In short, you've got much more potential to attract life's baddies if you are looking to be "fixed."

Unless you have self-esteem of steel and a strong sense of your own self-worth, you can be chipped away at bit by bit until you start to believe anything. That you're a bad person. That you're ugly. That you're somehow "to blame" for all the things that seem to go wrong in the relationship. That you deserve to be treated badly. That you eat picked onions the wrong way. Criticism can be as silly as that when you're with the wrong person. All relationships have their ups and downs, but the trick is knowing when something is just plain wrong.

Broken hearts do mend. I PROMISE. At the time, it feels like they never will, but they do.

How to Tell If Your Relationship Is Healthy or You NEED TO GET THE HELL OUT

Here are a few signs that I think mean you are in a healthy relationship:

You get along. This means that most of the time you actually like being together. You can tell the other person values your opinion. They look comfortable when they are with you. They may smile a lot. They are at ease.

You look comfortable when you are with them. You may smile a lot. You are at ease.

They want to share what they love with you AND they want to hear what you love. They will sit through your robust defense of trance music even though when they dance they look like Bambi on ice.

When they dance, you can say, "You dance like Bambi on ice," and they don't get hugely offended. That's because they know you love them and you know exactly what level of humor they can take. You don't feel you have to score cheap points by putting them down.

They let you shine. They support you. If you've got something you want to do, they work out a way with you to make it happen. If they think it's dangerous, they try to tell you why, with reasoned arguments. They never force themselves or their opinions on you. They may well think orange-flavored chocolate is a terrible thing, but they let you eat it without saying a word.

They never force themselves physically on you. No violence. Ever.

You always look forward to seeing them.

You don't have to pretend that you're something you are not. You can be the most authentic YOU there is. Good bits, bad bits, and the boring middle "I've got to finish this thing can you get me a Diet Coke, please" bits. They aren't freaked out by the way you eat pickled onions. No. I can't let that go.

Arguments and disagreements pass with both of you saying sorry if necessary. There's never any violence. Ever.

Sex is fun. For BOTH of you.

A GOOD RELATIONSHIP FEELS—

SAFE   LOVING

SUPPORTIVE

EQUAL

FUN

A Need-to-Get-the-Hell-Out! Relationship

Sometimes the most difficult thing about a get-the-hell-out relationship is getting the hell out. You may think you don't deserve to get out because you may have been sucked into viewing yourself as weak or horrible.

This is the key sign of a GET-THE-HELL-OUT relationship. You can't actually get the hell out! You feel stuck. You're going to need help with this. Talk to a friend. Talk to your doctor. Talk to one of the organizations at the back of this book. Find someone who can help you make the leap.

Other Signs You're in
an Abusive Relationship

Every time you see the other person, there's no excitement, just a lurch in your stomach. You don't know what mood they are going to be in—it may well be horrible.

You're not "you" when you're with them. You have to pretend to be a version of yourself. Or someone else.

They put you down. They tell you that there is something wrong with you or that you're ugly. They tell you no one else could love you. They criticize everything about you.

When you question them, they tell you YOU'RE "crazy." This is called "gaslighting." They manipulate you by lying or by claiming that you said or did something that YOU KNOW that you never did. Over time, their bullying makes you lose so much confidence in yourself that you feel more uncertain about facts. They make you doubt your beliefs about yourself and others. They make you question your sanity so you become more dependent on them.

They resent you spending time with other people. They try to isolate you from people you've known for years and/or from meeting new people.

They are also controlling. They want to know where you have been. They tell you what to wear and how you should look.

They bully you into sex or doing things during sex you don't feel comfortable with. They call you frigid if you don't want it as much as they do.

They think everything should be done a certain way and if it's not done their way it's totally WRONG. I was honestly not going to mention the onions here, but seriously if you're in the middle of a huge park and someone yells at you, "The way you eat pickled onions is wrong and disgusting," it's a very good example of what I'm talking about.

They tell you not to get ideas above your station. They tell you that you're "only fit" for a certain educational course/job and/or for a relationship with them.

They tell you that you couldn't survive without them. Unless you're a conjoined twin, this is not true of any other human being.

When you do something amazing that garners public acclaim, they find a way to bring you back into line. They abuse alcohol or drugs.

They are violent. They punch, kick, or spit at you. Sometimes it's in the middle of a fight. IT IS NEVER YOUR FAULT IF SOMEONE CANNOT CONTROL THEIR OWN TEMPER IF THEY ARE OVER THE AGE OF TWO.

They apologize, but then they do the same thing time and time again.

That little voice in your head is screaming that you need to get out, but you think you can't. You can and you must get out. Great people are out there. You don't deserve to feel bad. It's far better to be on your own than to be in a bad relationship.

Just to recap, BAD relationships make you feel:

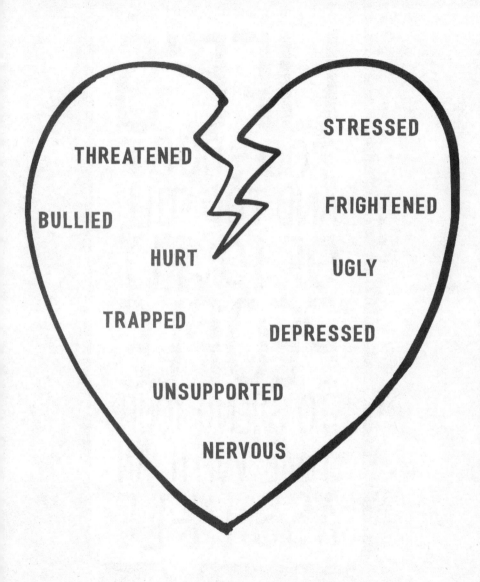

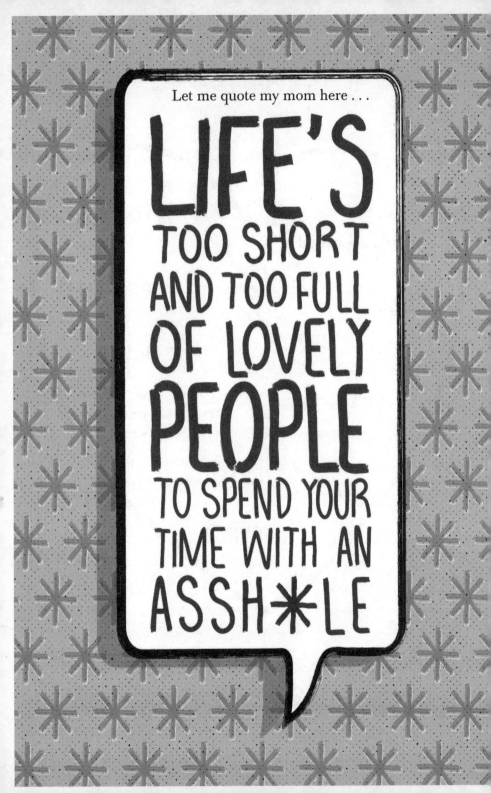

The Joys of Masturbation and Being Single

I cannot understand why more people, married or single, old or young, don't masturbate more often.

As a teenager, masturbation was the highlight of my week. I used to wait until my mom disappeared to my nan's house on a Sunday afternoon. I'd make sure she was past the phone box on Edinburgh Road (sometimes she came back to check the iron was off—OCD runs in families), I'd shut my bedroom curtains, and then off I'd go for an hour-long (AT LEAST) self-sex-fest. Undisturbed and glorious.

All you really need for masturbation is your imagination and a private space. As long as you don't use anything unsuitable in or around your body, it's completely safe, and it can give you a very strong indication of what you may or may not enjoy sexually. It's a really good way to test out your own brain. Pleasure mainly happens there, so it's good to get to know your own sex lobes. Actually I don't know if sex lobes really exist, but I DO know imagination can be responsible for mind-blowingly GREAT orgasms. There is near perfection in masturbation. It's your own private magnificent erotic world. It also relieves a shedload of stress.

Sometimes it can feel like everyone else is in a couple except you. If you're desperate for a relationship, you can feel like you must settle for the first thing that comes your way. This is a real mistake. Be choosy. When you are single, enjoy not having to think about anybody but yourself.

That's a pretty lovely state to be in. Someone WILL come along. In the meantime, get your head into the best state it can be in and indulge in some epic self-loving (best practiced once everyone else is out and if you have a room with a lock)!

"BUT SHE SAID THAT YOU SAID . . ."

Friendships

Good friends make life wonderful. They don't even have to try—they are sunshine on the cloudiest day and even more blistering golden sparkliness in the BEST moments.

Bad friendships can make you feel awful and can be detrimental to both your mental health and your entire life. It's not always easy to work out what is going on, though, and which is which. Good people can go bad. Previously average friends can turn out to be spectacularly better than first thought. Here are some tips to getting friendship right.

How to Be a Good Friend

Friendships have saved my life—and that is no exaggeration. I'm very lucky. I have had the greatest best friend in the history of time since I was sixteen. On top of that, I have some friends in my life who are like family. Even though I live far away from them, they manage, in their own special way, to make life better. When I think of how to be a good friend, I think about their qualities. This is what I think you want to be as a friend, and what I think you want from your friends:

Mort

Sometimes Mort and I don't get to speak for a while, but when we do, we pick up perfectly. My best friend and I have the most beautiful relationship. She is wise, she is funny, and she just loves all the bits of me. Mort has seen me at my very best and my very worst. She coped with a terrible panic attack I had in the middle of Poland twenty-six years ago. I could tell her everything then, and I can tell her everything now. She never judges, and she always tries to help. And I know if I rang her at two in the morning she'd be there for me. She's a linchpin in my life.

Lucy

My brilliant motivator in life, Lucy holds my hand as I do things I never thought I would. If I say to Lucy I want to do something, she will help me achieve it. She's as enthusiastic about my life as she is about her own. She believes in me even when I don't, and she encourages me to go beyond my comfort zone without going into my DANGER zone. I trust her opinion, and I trust that she always wants the best for me

Sazzy

Sazzy and I just slot together. You can tell her anything and she won't tell another soul. She's from my hometown but she's lived all over the world, so she understands how I feel about living abroad. We get on Skype and we don't stop laughing about things past and present. We've grown up together, we've changed together, and we still love each other.

Roo

I can chat to my super-smart, witty, and clever friend Roo for HOURS. We like a lot of the same things, and even though we didn't know each other until our twenties, we loved a lot of the same things growing up. We also have the same sense of humor. You need that sort of friend.

What Qualities Do All These People Have to Make Them Great Friends?

- They are all wise and willing to share their experiences.
- They have a fantastic sense of humor.
- They can keep a secret and honor my confidentiality.
- We have a shared history and a mutual trust.

- They aren't judgmental.
- We can be very silly together.
- They are great company.
- They are honest—they can tell it to me straight when necessary.
- They are enthusiastic and passionate.
- They have empathy for the situations I find my-self in.
- They are very loyal.
- If I put a laundry basket over my head while on Skype, each of them will accept it in their own unique way.

When I'm trying to be a good friend, I think about what my friends give me and I try to give it back. Friendship should always be a two-way street. You should be giving and getting. That's what I have with all these people. That's how I think great friendships are made.

How to Be a Really Bad Friend

Friendships can go bad for a whole variety of reasons. Often it's nobody's fault. You move away. You fall out over something silly and don't really manage to patch things up. You change. People change. You drift apart.

This isn't necessarily being a bad friend. I think it's just life. Sometimes, though, it's a lot more complicated than that. Good friendships can go bad, or good friends can go a bit rotten.

Here are some ways to be a bad friend:

Be mean. Put your friend down because you know they'll take it. This might be because you're feeling lousy, but it's still not right. Don't be there for your friend when they need you. Say you're too busy, too often.

Expect too much. Of course you want your friend to be there for you, but they can't fix everything. Don't get angry at them for this.

Get jealous. Of their life, their skills, their family, their other friends, their partner, or their new pedigree cocker spaniel Marmaduke Winslot Harbinger of Peace IV. Jealousy kills everything.

Make everything all about you. Hijack conversations. If your friend says, "I've hurt my knee," DON'T say, "I hurt my knee once. It really hurt. In fact, I think the time I hurt my knee the most was when I fell off a train once about THREE years ago . . ." Let people have their moment.

Steal their partner. Come on. You just don't.

Tell other people things your friend has told you in confidence.

Spread gossip about someone. Talk behind their back.

Sometimes we don't want to admit when we are being treated badly. It feels easier to let things carry on the way they are. The problem is, much like a bad romantic relationship, a bad friendship can be terrible for your mental health and self-esteem. You can't let someone's bad behavior carry on for too long without seriously considering whether the friendship is having a detrimental effect on your life.

When Friendships Go Wrong, and Accepting the End of a Friendship

When you know a friendship is going wrong, or simply not working for you, the best thing to do is to try to talk to the other person concerned. Don't do this over the phone or social media. I think to be done well and most effectively, it has to be done face-to-face and preferably with just you and your friend one on one. That way you can be really open and clear about what's going on in your head. Pick a neutral place. TOP RAE TIP—people are much less likely to kick off and shout in a public space, because they look like a total dick.

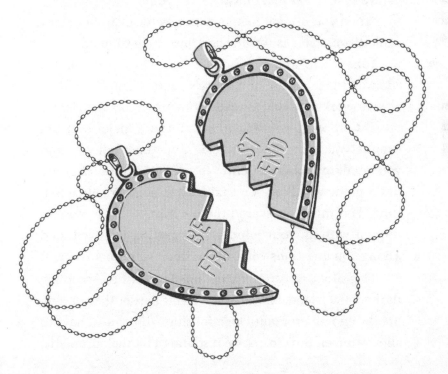

Try to stay calm and explain how you feel. It's good to write some notes about what you want to say before you go. (This works very well in lots of situations—always carry a notepad or write it down in your phone.) If you can, give specific examples of when things have not worked for you. Try to back up your feelings with facts. Explain that when your friend referred to you as someone who "ate like a big pig" in front of a person she knew you liked, it REALLY hurt your feelings and seemed like a deliberate attempt to bring you down.

(Yes, that did happen and no, it wasn't pickled onions. It was a hot vegetarian pizza with extra jalapeños, and how can you NOT eat that quickly, I ask you?)

When you present people with specific examples, they can't dismiss you as sensitive or "just imagining it."

Your friend may be genuinely surprised that you feel the way that you do, and there's every chance you'll be able to work out what is really going on and stay friends. Possibly, though, your friend may throw a major tantrum despite you being in Starbucks. They may tell you that you're talking total nonsense, storm out, and say they are never going to talk to you again. That can be really unsettling. You might be scared there's going to be a massive inquest with all your joint friends getting involved, and asking you questions you can't or don't want to answer.

This situation can be exceptionally stressful. Accepting the end of a friendship can often be far harder than accepting the end of a romantic relationship. You almost have to allow yourself time to grieve. It sounds a bit melodramatic, but anyone who has been through that experience knows it's very hard on your heart and your head.

Here are some tips that may stop the whole situation from turning into a massive drama:

- Tell people you don't want to talk about the situation. Chat about it with trusted friends, but leave it at that. People may talk about it for a time, but they'll soon move on. There'll be something else to talk about soon enough.

    - Write down what happened. Remind yourself why you had to question the friendship and why it came to an end.

- Don't turn the ex-friend into a huge villain figure in your life. It's a friendship that went wrong. They may have behaved badly, but try, if you can, to forgive them. It's hard, but hating someone is such a heavy burden to carry. I've gone FULL Oprah on you I know but it's true. There's an old Chinese proverb—"When you plan your revenge, first dig two graves." That's because keeping a massive grudge in your head is just not good for your mental health. Try to let it, and the person, go. Imagine waving them off at an airport, watching them go to another country. No. Don't imagine the plane crashing. Think nice thoughts.

- Tell mutual friends that you still want to be friends with them, and you don't want or expect them to choose sides.

- If your ex-friend takes it online and starts saying stuff about you on social media, don't get into a fight with them. Take a screen grab and tell someone—a parent, a teacher, or another adult you trust. Don't put up with things on your own either, though. You don't have to.

- Try to remember the good times. Your friend was your friend once for probably very good reasons. Unbelievably, but I have seen it happen, they may well be your friend again. Time is a great healer.

- Remind yourself that you are better off not having people in your life who aren't on your side, or who make you feel bad. Spend time with great friends. Remind yourself that you now have more time to be with people who really add something to your life. Great friends bring light to even the most dreadful time.

- Cry. Sob. Kick a piece of furniture. Smash something they bought you to smithereens. We all have an inner four-year-old. Let them loose in the privacy of your own home. There's no need to share it with anyone else except your wardrobe.

242

- If you are still feeling dreadful about it after a few weeks, talk to a person you trust. We've all been through it at some stage in our lives, and someone may be able to help.

- Some friendships can last for decades, or even a lifetime. Some people pass in and out of your life without much drama but leave lovely memories behind them. Occasionally, someone sets off a crap bomb of emotions in your head. When that bomb goes off, remember most people in your life are wonderful, and seek shelter with them. Your head will get better and your heart will heal. Been there. Done it. Got a sore toe from kicking the wardrobe.

"AREN'T FRENCH FRIES FUNNY?!"

Drugs and Alcohol

In the late nineties, my good friend Andrew summed up one problem with illegal drugs very well. "Rae," he said, "I don't want to take anything that someone may have smuggled into this country by sticking it up their ass."

This is a very good point, but it isn't the only problem with drugs.

New drugs appear on the market every week. There are legal and illegal highs. Some people use prescription medication or a combination of alcohol and drugs to get high. Some people can take drugs, particularly recreational drugs like ecstasy, and seemingly get away with it with no long-term ill effects at all.

However, if you've ever had a mental health problem, or you take your mental health seriously, you're going to have to think long and hard before taking anything. Sorry to sound dull—but it's true.

This is because all drugs present the same problem. When you take them, you mess with the delicate chemical balance in your brain. How one drug affects one person isn't necessarily how it's going to affect another. I can prove this with my first experience with marijuana.

At my university a group of us decided it would be a fabulous idea to make hash cakes. I know that sounds lame, and a bit *The Great British Drug Off*, but it was the nineties— this sort of thing happened. Hash cakes were basically a batch of chocolate brownies with a special ingredient— dope. I'd never had marijuana before and I thought it was a really gentle drug—a bit like moldy lager. I ate the cake, and about an hour later everyone else started laughing at stuff. Windshield wipers were hilarious. French fries were funny. I wasn't feeling very funny, though. I was feeling very odd. It wasn't a nice odd either, so I slipped away back to my bedroom.

Back in my room, I started to slip through space and time. Not really, of course. I'm not Doctor Who. I was just off my face, and my brain couldn't handle it. Every time I closed my eyes, I was falling through the universe. Meanwhile everyone else was having loads of cheese and tomato toasted sandwiches and giggling at lampshades.

Life and drugs are not fair.

I realized when I was back on planet Earth that I just wasn't capable of handling illegal drugs. Thus, during my

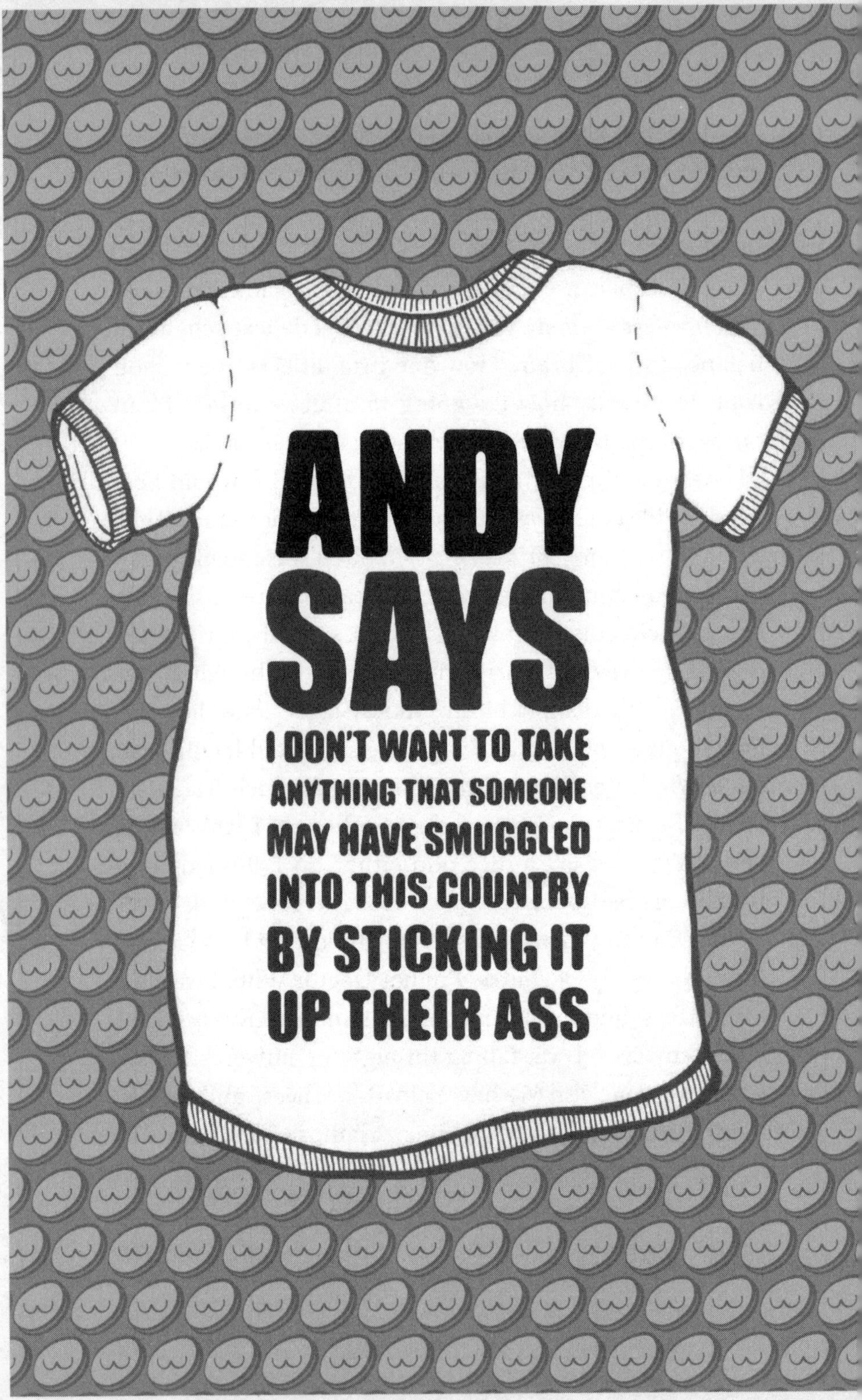
ANDY
SAYS
I DON'T WANT TO TAKE
ANYTHING THAT SOMEONE
MAY HAVE SMUGGLED
INTO THIS COUNTRY
BY STICKING IT
UP THEIR ASS

entire time at college, and during the peak years of rave, I never took one solitary E. Nor LSD, cocaine, speed, or anything else. I felt I just couldn't risk it. My thinking was that one amazing night out was not worth the risk of a spell back in a psychiatric ward. Financially, I couldn't afford to take another year off from my education, and I didn't want to mess up again. Now I can say I have never regretted this decision. The stakes were just too high for me. My sanity was hard-fought.

And drugs are very unpredictable. I made the decision not to partake because I didn't want a relapse or a bad reaction to a drug. I'm too highly strung. I hate that phrase, but in my case, it's true.

You've got the same decision to make. The truth is, with every drug there's a risk. We know that prolonged marijuana use may make some people more susceptible to schizophrenia. Any drug has the potential to cause a long-term mental health problem. We just don't know.

Drug dealers are, in the main, very money-oriented. They don't give a monkey about your mental health. I don't think they'd argue with that. Jacuzzis with disco lights are more important to them than your sanity. They care about profit. That's why they're in the business. With illegal drugs, you really don't know what you're getting. With legal drugs and medicines, even simple over-the-counter drugs like acetaminophen (Tylenol) and aspirin have been through a multitude of tests. Illegal drugs, on the other hand, could be made up of any old nonsense just to maximize the money the dealer makes.

You could be throwing a great deal at your brain all

in one go. It's a finely tuned engine. If it needs drugs, it needs finely tuned drugs, not something that's cut with talcum powder or other random crap someone found in their bathroom or kitchen cupboard.

Alcohol also presents real challenges. It may be legal to drink IF YOU ARE OVER TWENTY-ONE, but it's a known depressant. Binge drinking or drinking to excess can knock your head out of whack really easily. Also, if you are taking any kind of psychiatric medication, you should NOT be drinking at all. Trust me—meds and booze do not go together.

> **Dr. R. says:** *We know that mixing alcohol and drugs can exacerbate the already dangerous effects of both and increase the risk of fatalities.*

I've drunk to excess and made a total ass of myself in so many ways they could form a separate book. It's almost certain that at some stage, you may do the same. Please eat before you go out, stay with your friends, and never get so plastered that you don't know where you are or what you're doing. French fries on the way home are good.

Addiction

Put simply, addiction means that your brain and body can't imagine life without the "drug" you're addicted to. When people say addiction, most of us think of an addiction to drink or drugs. However, it's possible to get addicted to many things, from gambling to social media use. "Drugs" come in all shapes and sizes.

You may feel like you rely on your drug to get you through each day, or to feel "normal." Many people use their drug of choice to self-medicate through mental health problems, because they've been unable to get adequate care or been too ashamed to get help. Some drugs are physically addictive, some are psychologically addictive, and some are both. Dr. R. will explain the difference:

> *Physical addiction is when your body reacts because it is withdrawing (not getting enough of) the chemical substance in the drug you have been taking. You experience physical symptoms from this lack of the chemical. These can be really distressing and unpleasant, and so people take more of the chemical to avoid them. Psychological addiction is when you become mentally dependent on a drug and you get symptoms related to your thoughts and emotions, like intense cravings, anxiety, depression, or irritability. So these feelings and thoughts make you continue to use the drug.*

If you do have an addiction problem, you need specialist help. It's almost impossible to fight addiction on your own, and you shouldn't have to. At the back of this book is a list of organizations that can help you, including the brilliant website FRANK, which talks about all sorts of drugs with FACT not opinion. Your first port of call, though, should definitely be your doctor. Be totally honest with them. Addictions are a very common issue, and your doctor will almost certainly have dealt with a problem like yours before.

"IT'S FOR YOUR OWN GOOD!"

Parents

The truth about parenting.

Now that I am a parent, I can tell you the absolute truth of parenting. I'm telling you this because it may help you understand your own mom and dad more.

Parenting is utterly, utterly terrifying. Here's what happens. You have sex, feel a bit odd a few weeks later, and then all hell breaks loose. When you finally do give birth, you have some time in the hospital and then THEY ACTUALLY SEND YOU HOME WITH IT. You can't believe they are letting you do it. It's insane. My coffeemaker came with more instructions. You can read manuals, but babies don't bother reading them with you.

Being a Parent Is Terrifying.
We Are Making It Up as We Go Along.

Also, you love this thing that's exploded into your life more than anything else, yet you are meant to let it out of your sight sometimes. It's all insane. And then you are meant to let it do stuff on its own and make its own mistakes and get hurt and, oh—it's a hugely flawed system. I'd like to change it.

Basically being a parent is the best thing and the most scary thing all at the same time.

Please remember that when a parent is giving you grief. I have to and I'm forty-five. The other day, my mom told someone I have tantrums. I don't. I do get cross, but to my mom I will forever be the three-and-a-half-year-old lying down in the middle of Stamford High Street crying about the demise of my DIY Scotch tape dog. I have to let it go. She's a parent—SHE CAN'T HELP IT.

What I'm saying is that a good start to a better relationship with your parents is to try (I know it's tough) to remember they are HUMAN. Like you. They won't always get it right, but hopefully, if they are a half-decent parent, they will really be trying to do their best for you.

Identify the Breed of Parent You've Adopted

Parents come in many different shapes and sizes. Your family setup may have one parent, or many parents. There are lots of ways to be a good parent and many ways to be a lousy one. Identifying what breed of parent you have will help you have the best relationship with them. You'll know how to train them and how to treat them.

Unbelievable Labradoodle

They are just lovely to be around. You can tell them everything. You can say what you like to them. You get along with them, and they trust you to make your own mistakes. They are always there for you when you've got a problem, and they fully respect your decisions and choices.

If you've got this parent, you are lucky. Perhaps your behavior has allowed them to be like this. Carry on the way you are. Please just remember to buy them treats every so often to reward their brilliance.

Alsatian

Alsatians are lovely, but they are much more snappy and protective than the Unbelievable Labradoodle. They may be far stricter about what they think you should be doing or not doing, and may be defensive about the friends you have or the partners you choose. The thing to remember is, they are guarding your best interests. Give them plenty of information and reassurance, and let them bark at people you bring round to your house. It doesn't hurt for other people to know you're well looked after. Alsatian parents may occasionally snap, but it's done out of love.

Don't try to change them. Try to enjoy how much they want to protect you.

Rabid Dog of Doom

You are fighting night and day. It's like they've been put on this earth to give you hell. They moan at you constantly. You can't do a thing right. They wake up barking at you and they tut about your behavior in their sleep. It's like walking on eggshells constantly. If you have a parent like this, it's good to ask what has gone wrong. Getting someone else involved at this stage is a great idea— you could try a teacher, a counselor, or a trusted family member. A Rabid Dog of Doom will often calm down in an environment with another trained adult.

Crossbreed

Most parents are a mixture of all these dogs. You'll find that often-personal circumstances and situations decide what breed you get on any given day. What you do, and how you react to what's going on in your life, will also affect how your parents treat you.

As long as you have a parent who loves you and isn't being abusive, you've got something to work with. Don't stop talking to each other. Even bickering is better than nothing at all—as my mom and I prove every time we are together.

I love her, though. She just annoys me. If you're feeling

similar, that's a totally normal reaction to both pets and parents. It's more common with parents.

Communicating with Your Parent

If there is something I have learned over the years it's that communicating with parents can be hard. This is because even when you are trying to be completely sensible and honest they may still have a tendency to get really angry in a frankly unreasonable way. I say this as someone who had an argument with their mother yesterday about how to chop lettuce properly. I wish I was joking. The FOUR key things to remember about parents are—

1. THEY LOVE YOU SO MUCH THEY WOULD PROBABLY DIE FOR YOU.

2. THEY DON'T WANT YOU TO DO ANYTHING THAT MIGHT HURT YOU.

3. THEY ARE PROBABLY JUST TRYING TO HELP.

4. THEY CAN'T HELP BEING IDIOTS SOMETIMES. THEY ARE SADLY CURSED WITH BEING HUMAN LIKE THE REST OF US.

If you do want to talk to your parents about something important, I've discovered that preparation is key. Pick a time when they are relaxed. After they've eaten in the evening but not in the middle of their favorite show. (I disturbed *Midsomer Murders* once. I won't do that again.) Make sure you know what you want to say. Write down some key points to help you as you talk. If you've got a lot to talk about, it's easy to lose your train of thought. If you've thought about what you are going to say, you'll be able to express what you're thinking and feeling more clearly.

If your parent reacts badly to what you are saying, try not to get pulled into an argument with them. Leave the room (don't diva-exit) and remove yourself from the situation until things have calmed down. Sometimes you have to let people be angry and have their moment. After that you can sort things out.

If you've done something stupid, take responsibility for it. Telling someone you've done something dumb and you need help with the situation will make most of us melt. That's because we've ALL done something stupid. We GET it.

Don't forget your parents love you. They want to stop you from experiencing any pain at all. The fact they cannot do this might sometimes make them react in a somewhat unhelpful way. Even if you feel like going ballistic, try to give them a break.

How to Cope with a Parent or Family Member with a Mental Health Issue

When a parent or family member has a mental health issue, it can be very difficult to cope with. Even though you know that person is not to blame for their illness, you may feel overwhelmed, irritated, angry, sad, guilty, or embarrassed. You may also feel terrible for thinking these things in the first place. I know I have. I also said some really selfish, unhelpful things to my mom when I was younger.

The key thing to remember is that there's a huge difference between thinking and doing something. Thoughts can stay in your head and run free in your brain. You're entitled to feel how you feel. It's how you manage those feelings and what you do with them that matters.

A good thing to do is to research as much as you can about the mental illness your family member has. Many mental health problems are supported through organizations that can offer you real help and understanding. Sometimes you just want someone to KNOW what you're going through. People who have been through a similar situation can offer help and advice. They will also let you say things that sound unhelpful or even horrible without judging you. They've been there. They get it.

It's a balancing act really. It's wonderful to be able to support someone with a mental health problem, but you must make sure you look after yourself too. When you're well, you're in the best position to help your family and loved ones—and everyone else in the world generally.

Having a family member with certain mental health

conditions can also make you more likely to develop a condition yourself. This isn't something to be scared of, but it IS something to be aware of. I'm going to hand over to Dr. R. to explain a bit more:

> *For example, having a family member who has been affected by alcohol dependency is a risk factor for developing problematic alcohol use in the future. Often if a parent has had alcohol dependency, this can affect family members. Children often become the "carer" for their parent and they put their needs after their parent's. As adults, these children can find they have low self-esteem, difficulties in expressing their needs, and trust difficulties with relationships.*

To summarize this chapter, I think it's worth repeating our "parent mantra" here. PLEASE remember:

Parent Mantra

1. THEY LOVE YOU SO MUCH THEY WOULD PROBABLY DIE FOR YOU.

2. THEY DON'T WANT YOU TO DO ANYTHING THAT MIGHT HURT YOU.

3. THEY ARE PROBABLY JUST TRYING TO HELP.

4. THEY CAN'T HELP BEING IDIOTS SOMETIMES. THEY ARE SADLY CURSED WITH BEING HUMAN LIKE THE REST OF US.

Dealing with an Abusive Parent

If you have an abusive parent, I am so sorry. You don't deserve it. Let me tell you straight, nothing you have done and nothing you could ever do will change their behavior.

NONE OF THIS IS YOUR FAULT.
NONE OF IT.

You're not responsible for what they do. If they've told you otherwise, you've been let down very badly. They've lied to you. You deserve and are going to need lots of help so that YOU can survive and thrive despite the lousy start you've had. The good news is

ALL THE REST OF US KNOW THAT WHAT IS HAPPENING TO YOU IS WRONG.

We want to help, but we need to know what's going on.

Abusive people can be very manipulative. They may have told you that you can't tell anyone what's happening to you. There is no such thing as a secret you can't tell one other person you trust. It may be that you feel telling someone else would be disloyal to your parent (you may well still love the person who's abusing you) or you've been threatened with something dreadful if you tell someone. Please, we NEED to hear your story. No one wants you to suffer.

You're in a dreadfully unfair situation and we want to help you get out of it so you can have the best life possible.

Your parent may well have a problem that, when fixed, makes them a better human being and a better parent. That's not your problem. THAT IS THEIR PROBLEM. Your issue and our issue is YOU. Please speak up.

> **Dr. R. says:** *You may want to tell a trusted teacher, school counselor, or an aunt or uncle. There is always an adult you can find to tell. Your doctor is also there for you if you need, and all of these adults care about you and want you to be physically and emotionally safe.*

"I SWEAR I WILL NEVER EVER SAY 'PULL YOURSELF TOGETHER' OR 'COME ON, GIVE ME A SMILE'"

Helping Someone with a Mental Illness

We've touched on this elsewhere in the book, but it's worth tackling the subject in detail. Mental illness is not rare, and it's very likely you know someone who is suffering, or has suffered, with one.

Helping someone with a mental illness is like helping someone with any illness—different things work better for different people. When I'm not feeling mentally well, I HAVE to walk with music. I have to leave the house and STOMP it out. For lots of people, treading the streets to "Strong" by London Grammar would be a useless thing to do, but it makes me feel 1,000 percent better. It's difficult then, when a friend or family member is unwell, to know what to do. Perhaps it's easier to start with a list of don'ts. These are universally unhelpful things to do or say to anyone that's suffering with a mental illness:

Don't try to solve all their problems. I'm a terrible fixer. I want to make everyone feel better. The truth is, I can't, and I often annoy people trying. Honestly sometimes it's more about MY discomfort with someone's illness than their discomfort. I'm actually trying to fix that. That's wrong.

Don't be the clown who tries to make them smile or the advice-giver who tries to wave a magic wand over their illness and their life. That isn't helping them. Honor where someone is in their life, and listen.

Don't tell them to pull themselves together, or to smile. As a general rule, if you wouldn't say it to someone with acute appendicitis, don't say it to someone with a mental illness.

Encourage them to seek professional help, but don't moan at them. Sometimes going on and on about getting help may make someone feel pressured and stressed and perhaps less likely to get help.

Don't hover over them like a hawk or smother them. Obviously if you think they are suicidal, you should seek professional help as soon as you can. But if it's an on-going, less urgent condition that's being managed, be there for them without continually pelting them with affection.

There are some very simple ways you can help someone with their mental health:

Be a good listener. Lots of people think they listen, but they don't. They are actually thinking about how they are feeling and what they are going to say next. That's a different thing. Just try listening. Let the person say how they feel and what's going on in their head.

Tell the person that you'll support them in any way that you can, and then do what you can. You don't need to promise them the world—just do what you can. Follow through on anything you suggest and let them know they can rely on you.

Still suggest doing the normal stuff—going to the movies or binge-watching Netflix at home. Accept that the answer to what you're suggesting may be no, but don't stop trying to include that person in your life. Sometimes an invitation is enough to help someone realize that they are being thought of and cared for.

Remind them that you can recover from mental illness or learn to control and manage your condition. This is such an important message. When you're in the grips of something awful in your head, it's often very difficult to see even a tiny chink of light or a way forward. Be the person who opens the curtains and lets a bit of sunshine in. Send them stuff in the post even if they live in the same house. No—it doesn't cure mental illness, but it MIGHT give someone a tiny chink of silly light. We all need that sometimes.

How to Help Yourself When You're Helping Others

If you're helping someone with a mental illness, you STILL need to look after yourself.

Let's go right back to the beginning, and my suggestion that you should:

Put your own oxygen mask on before helping others

That's even more important in a situation when you're helping someone with a mental illness. You need to make sure that you aren't drowning in someone else's life. In the past, I've certainly been guilty of concentrating on other people's issues and ignoring my own. It's easy to feel overwhelmed and to start "caring" disproportionately—so much so that it affects your health. Compassion fatigue is a very real thing.

Sometimes people with mental illnesses can be challenging to be with. They may make you feel frustrated, angry, upset, or scared. They may be manipulative and unpleasant at times. They are still human beings after all. The key thing to remember is that your mental health matters too. If you feel that it's all getting too much, have someone you trust in your life that you can talk to. They can help you to decide on the best course of action.

Looking after our mental health is a lifelong commitment. It's a commitment that ensures YOU have the best time possible on this earth. Always make time to check that your "oxygen mask" hasn't slipped off. Keep checking that. It's vitally important because YOU are vitally important.

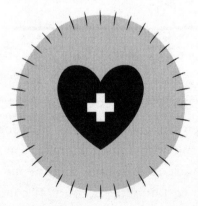

MY MINI LIFE MANIFESTO OF REALLY IMPORTANT FACTS

Most of us are muddling through. You get more experienced and stylish at muddling through with practice but it's still . . . muddling.

1. You don't have to talk to people who want to talk to you on public transportation—especially late at night. Keep your earphones in and make up your own foreign language if you need to. Music is a sacred thing. You don't have to talk to strangers on trains/buses/planes.

2. Melon is not a legitimate appetizer. I don't think it should be a real food.

3. Wear what you like. Don't let your size, age, shape, or anyone else's opinion about your size, age, or shape make a difference in what you wear. THEY ARE JUST CLOTHES. HAVE FUN.

4. So little really matters. Work out what matters to you and make sure you do that well.

5. Sometimes it's fine to "phone it in." Some days have to be survived.

6. When everyone else is quiet, it's fine to be loud. When everyone else is loud, it's fine to be quiet.

7. Don't cook avocado. Ever.

8. If you get a dry nervous mouth, gently bite the end of your tongue.

9. Cats are ALWAYS in control. Don't kid yourself.

10. There was never a golden, simpler time in life. Every generation has different challenges to cope with. A lot of people think the world was simpler when they were young. No it wasn't. It was just simpler for THEM. Nostalgia always paints the past in a golden glow. We often forget the bad times. I had a mammoth music session on YouTube the other day. I listened to every era from about 1975 onward. Under each video somebody had written something like "This reminds me of a simpler time." Don't let yourself be convinced that your present is all doom and gloom. It's not.

11. That reminds me—avoid reading YouTube comments.

12. Learn how to argue and debate without losing your temper. It's one of the most important life skills they don't always teach you in school.

Probably because you're dangerous when you're good at it.

13. Don't discount being friends with people who have different political views from you—unless they're a Nazi. Don't bother with them.

14. If it's not hurting you or anyone else, it's not a guilty pleasure. It's just a pleasure.

15. Good underwear never features the word "string."

16. If seven Russians tell you you're drunk, lie down. Basically if lots of people are telling you the same thing, at least consider they may have a point. *OMG. Is that offensive? I just want to say not all Russians drink. It's just a phrase.*

17. Never go to bed still arguing. Better to stay up late and sort it out.

18. If something isn't working when you've tried everything to make it work—let it go. That's not quitting. That's common sense.

19. Don't have one dream. It's too risky. Have lots. Your brain can take it.

20. Be kind to pigeons. They are super smart and just doing their best surviving thing.

21. Poetry is the superfood snack of literature. It doesn't take up much of your time, but it gives you lots of head nourishment.

22. Duvets and their covers are annoying. I've switched to blankets and never looked back.

23. You can't have enough pens.

24. Time heals a great deal if you let it.

25. There are loads of ways to make a mess but even more ways to make amends.

Dr. Pop

When I used to work in an office, we spent a lot of time talking crap. However, some of this crap was actual genius. My friend Andy and I created something called DR. POP PRESCRIBES. This is because we were convinced we could heal most people's problems and, indeed, the problems of the entire world, with music.

We would tell each other how we felt and then Dr. Pop (us) would prescribe a song to ease that ill, make a bad mood good, and make a good mood even better.

With this in mind, I'd like to share some of Dr. Pop's all-time favorite tunes for better mental health. Music and dancing release a chemical called dopamine in your brain that makes you happy, so there's some real science behind Dr. Pop. It is NOT just the silly creation of two bored people who love music.

"Ain't Got No, I Got Life"—Nina Simone
Starts off as the most depressing song ever as Nina goes through in detail what she does not have, but THEN! Well, listen. By the end you're like YEAH—I'M ALIVE.

"Straight Lines"—Silverchair
Written about lead singer Daniel John's recovery from an eating disorder and depression. The lyrics are JUST BEAUTIFUL, the music glorious, and the instruction simple—just take life step by step and move forward.

"Dancing Queen"—ABBA

Oh, it just makes you feel GOOD.

"Happy Endings"—Pulp

If you're in the middle of a messy breakup, this song acknowledges all your pain yet gives you a bit of hope. It kills me every time I listen to it.

"Badhead"—Blur

For "phone it in" days. For those days you just have to get through.

"Shout"—Tears for Fears

It's angry. Great song to walk to.

"Rise"—PIL

For when you've seen the news and you're feeling really angry at the world. IT IS RIGHTEOUS FURY. Perfect for running.

"Café del mar (Michael Woods Remix)"
—Energy 52

This is how to chill out. The Michael Woods remix of "Café del mar" gave me a deeply spiritual experience on a plane over Australia once. I started to cry at the beauty of everything and the steward came over to see if I was OK. I was. How to explain that the mixture of beautiful music and looking at a storm in the distance had brought me nearer to the meaning of my life? I didn't bother. I just said I was homesick. I wasn't. I was HEALED BY TUNE.

"Hit Me with Your Rhythm Stick"
—Ian Dury and the Blockheads
All I can say is I have never listened to this song and not felt a tiny bit better by the end of it.

"Mr. Blue Sky"—ELO
Another song that just brings me joy. But then there's that orchestral end that makes me sob wonderful fat tears. When you want to FEEL.

"Champagne Supernova"—Oasis
For a moment you want to capture. A magnificent time with your friends. It makes that moment glittery and mammoth. Let it run all the way through, though. Speaking of which . . .

"Heroes"—David Bowie
When he sings it, I believe him. I feel braver.

"Walk Away"—Cast
When you know you've had enough of a situation or of a person. You know you've got to make a change. This song tells you you're fine and you're going to be OK.

"Point of View"—DB Boulevard
Yes, it is a jolly little dance song, but actually it's also about flipping your thinking. A brain and a foot mover.

"The Power of Love"
—Frankie Goes to Hollywood
If there's a lovelier song to remind you how beautiful love is and to feed your very soul, I can't think of it right now. And my pop memory is long . . .

"A Bad Dream"—Keane
The best song for the tired and bewildered.
Honors where you are and doesn't try to fix it.
Just empathizes.

"Bring Me Sunshine"—Morecambe and Wise
For when you need something simple and wonderful to give you a lift.

"My World"—Secret Affair
For when you need reminding that this is YOUR life.
People can talk but you've got to do YOUR thing.

"We Are the Champions"—Queen
For every victory you have in your life. Even if it's just running for the bus and not falling over.

"Miracle"—Tom Baxter
Reminds you that amazing things can happen, but you've got to make them happen and YOU CAN.

This is just a tiny selection from the Dr. Pop surgery. I am now buzzing and wanting to get away from my laptop for a frankly obscene music binge.

All these are just suggestions. Please find tunes that heal you—they are out there. It doesn't matter what type of music it is. All music reaches parts of the brain that other things cannot touch. Not even language. Get on YouTube and explore. Everyone is a Dr. Pop. Everyone can help themselves get better.

Organizations That Can Help You Get Better

This is by no means a complete list, but here are some organizations that exist to help you with your mental health. Lots of them have many ways to get in touch. If you don't feel like talking, you don't have to. You can type if you want to.

headstogether.org.uk
Heads Together wants people to start conversations about mental illness. They have some really inspiring stories on their site that might help you to explain how you are feeling to someone you love.

They are also supported by Prince Harry. This has automatically made them my mom's favorite charity in history.

ocdaction.org.uk
Fantastic charity that explains all the different types of OCD in depth and helps you to cope and live with the condition. A really good website to show someone who thinks OCD is just about being "clean and tidy."

samaritansusa.org
Open 24 hours a day, 7 days a week, 365 days a year. Access to some of the kindest and best-trained listeners in the world. They saved my sanity. They could help you save yours

talktofrank.com/drugs-a-z
FRANK is a magnificent website that goes through every possible drug and tells you both the effects and the risks associated with it. It's not preachy. It's factual.

youngminds.org.uk
Young Minds wants you to know you're not alone and you deserve to be heard. That's all many of us need to hear. Their website is a fantastic place to start.

youth.anxietybc.com
Anxiety can really suck. They understand. Packed with practical advice and resources that will really help.

nationaleatingdisorders.org/help-support
A comprehensive guide to all kinds of eating disorders and how to recover from them.

Brilliant Books

Anxiety Sucks! A Teen Survival Guide
by Natasha Daniels
Create Space Independent Publishing (2016)

**A Still Quiet Place for Teens: A Mindfulness
Workbook to Ease Stress and Difficult Emotions**
by Amy Saltzman
New Harbinger (2014)
A great introduction into mindfulness meditation to help
manage stress and anxiety for teens.

**Conquer Negative Thinking for Teens: A
Workbook to Break the Nine Thought Habits
That Are Holding You Back**
by Mary Karapetian
Alvord Instant Help (2017)

**My Anxious Mind: A Teen's Guide to Managing
Anxiety and Panic**
by Michael A. Tompkins and Katherine Martinez
American Psychological Association (2010)
Discusses common anxieties, and outlines several tools and
techniques for dealing with phobias, anxieties, and panic
attacks.

**Outsmarting Worry: An Older Kid's Guide to
Managing Anxiety**
by Dawn Huebner, PhD
Jessica Kingsley Publishers (2017)

Apps

Apps can also be a really useful tool to support your recovery.

Anxiety Coach is a self-help app that addresses fears and worries using cognitive and behavioral strategies.

Anxiety Reliever is an app that enables users to track anxiety symptoms and provides relaxation exercises.

Breathe2Relax teaches breathing techniques to manage stress.

Happify is a self-guided app that aims to increase positive emotions through exercises and games supported by positive psychology and mindfulness research.

Headspace teaches meditation to reduce anxiety and stress, and improve attention and awareness.

iCounselor OCD is an app designed to teach users skills to help them with OCD symptoms.

Live OCD Free offers cognitive and behavioral tools, including support with exposure response prevention exercises, for OCD.

Pacifica teaches deep breathing, behavioral exercises, and exercises for identifying cognitive distortions (negative thinking patterns) and learning how to replace them with positive thinking patterns.

T2 Mood Tracker helps individuals track their emotional states and how they change over time for personal insight and accurate reporting to a mental health professional.

INDEX

About the Author

Rae Earl was born in Stamford, Lincolnshire, in England. After graduating from Hull University, she did every job in a radio station except "accountant." Rae has written articles for *The Guardian*, *Marie Claire*, and *Elle*, and she has been featured in *The Telegraph* and *The Times*, among others. She has also appeared on BBC Breakfast TV, BBC World Service, and countless local radio stations. Her books *My Mad Fat Diary* and *My Madder Fatter Diary* have been made into a TV show that is shown in over fifty countries worldwide, including the USA. *My Life Uploaded* is coming out in spring 2018. She currently lives in Hobart, Tasmania, with her husband and son.